Understanding Poems Of the Decade for AS level Edexcel Poetry

Gavin's Guide to the 28 set poems for 2017 & 2018 students

By Gavin Smithers

Another of **Gavin's Guides** – study books packed with insight. They aim to help you raise your grade!

"Understanding Poems of the Decade for AS level Edexcel Poetry" is a complete study guide, written for students and teachers who are preparing for AS level exams in 2017 and subsequent years.

Series Editor: Gill Chilton

1

The complete text of "Poems of the Decade An anthology of the Forward Books of Poetry" is published by Forward in association with Faber & Faber and is widely available. You will need a copy of this book to use alongside this study guide.

CONTENTS

FACING THE CHALLENGE

The examining board Edexcel has chosen 28 out of 105 poems that comprise Poems of the Decade An anthology of the Forward Books of Poetry. The subset of 28 that they have selected- all published since the year 2000- is a challenging and stimulating choice for students.

If you are taking AS levels from 2017 and have these as part of your exam – then I would say that is excellent news. It is in having challenging material that you can stretch yourself during the course (and come to love literature and poetry that bit more) AND you can also show off your expertise to achieve a truly good grade.

The Forward poems are new to the specification and were examined for the first time in 2016. So at time of writing, there are yet to be any published results. Following different set texts, in 2015, 5,112 students took the Edexcel AS English Literature exam. 21% were awarded A grades; a further 28% Bs; and another 28% Cs

If, you are reading this some weeks and months into your course, then, as an AS student, you will already have noticed a huge shift in what is expected from you as a student of poetry.

At GCSE level, the poetry is generally much simpler to analyse; think Wilfred Owen and the war poets and moving, yet clear themes. Here, in this anthology, the key difference is the level of ambiguity.

This makes for a more complex poem...and a more complex response required from you, the student who wishes to achieve a good grade.

In particular, contemporary poetry is likely to be less formal and less constrained than the "literary heritage" element that you may be familiar with from GCSE; for A level, we can expect to encounter the most diverse and creative range of forms and structures.

This demands, from us, as readers, an open mind and a disciplined and methodical critical approach. What I ask is that you bring the first element of that – and let this guide help you with the second. Then, all you need is a few clear hours and a copy of the anthology to hand as you read this Gavin's Guide.

KEY FEATURES OF THE POEMS

Of the 28 poems, only eight use rhyme in a traditional way. This means that, even at the most fundamental level, 20 of the poems are unconventional.

Within the large group you study, we find some poems with strict formal regularity in the use of stanzas; preferences for stanzas of 2, 3 or 4 or 5 lines, or any combination of those; the use of a single stanza for a whole poem, and the use of a one-line stanza.

Within these poems, you will find words, objects and conditions such as a noyade, a cithara, and chlamydia- a dazzling range of linguistic play and virtuosity, some haunting images and a wide variety of behaviours and emotions.

Family relationships are examined from the point of view of both parents and children, often uncomfortably. Loneliness, illness, disability and death (sometimes violent death) feature. But so does the exuberance of youth, and the excitement of growing up and into adulthood. The real meets the surreal. The past invades the present. The world shrinks and expands.

You may cry and smile and laugh; admire, criticise; recognise yourself and people you know, or think you know.

You cannot read and live with these poems and fail to become a more humane and civilised human being.

This is the joy and the essence of good poetry.

<u>The fact is, though, that you are reading these poems not because they are good for you but because you will be subjecting them to a process of literary criticism.</u>

Specifically, you will be required to comment on the poets' themes (what the poems are about; their meaning); their use of language and imagery (why the poets make the linguistic choices they do; what resonates with you, and why and how it does); and their use of "other poetic techniques"- a catch-all which includes form and structure, symbolism, context, irony, ambiguity.

Please do not be daunted by such a tall set of tasks. Think back to the start of Y10, when the GSCE syllabus seemed daunting also. At A level, candidates have a very obvious advantage: they have actively chosen to pursue the subject.

WHAT THIS GAVIN'S GUIDE CAN DO

I am both a private tutor and a parent of someone who is studying these poems. I tutor English because

I have a passion for the subject. I hope that this Gavin's Guide will be able to pass on some of that enthusiasm for the shaped word to you.

There is little published analysis yet available for "Poems of the Decade", it seems; and I am not aware of a concise guide to all the poems in the collection for Edexcel, in a single volume, at a competitive price. Hence this guide!

I do not aim to provide a comprehensive, encyclopaedic analysis here. Your readings and responses will quite probably be very different from mine, because your background, values and experiences are uniquely your own, just as mine are mine!

What I will do is **give you relevant intertextual information, and introduce you to a sound critical method which you can adapt and extend for yourself**.

This guide is designed to help you bridge the gap from GCSE analysis to the deeper analysis AS/A level requires.

I believe that our conclusions should first and foremost be grounded in the text, so you will find a strong emphasis here on language.

We must also allow the poem the time and space it needs to work on us as a spontaneous experience, pay due regard to our own emotional response, and read and reread until we come to a settled understanding and interpretation. Don't expect that to happen overnight! A poem may be few in words –but studying it well is seldom swift.

YOUR TASK AHEAD

Here's a quick reminder of the format of the question you will be set for AS-

Explore the ways in which poets explore (theme/ universal themes) in poem x and one other poem of your choice.

You should consider the poets' development of themes; use of language and imagery; other poetic techniques.

So, now for the analysis!

Patience Agbabi   Eat Me

This poem manages to be darkly comic and disturbing at the same time. It appears, on first reading, to be about the narrator's birthdays, but a more accurate reading derives from the repetition of the word **fat** six times in the seventh stanza.

Thirty is the measurement of BMI (body mass index) at which we become not overweight but clinically obese, and at risk of a range of debilitating illnesses and diseases, as a result of choosing to eat too much and exercise too little.

The poem – like this critical BMI number- comprises **thirty** lines (ten stanzas of three lines each). **Thirty-nine** is the BMI figure at the upper limit of the obese range; at a BMI of **forty**, we become morbidly obese. The male figure in this poem looks forward to the point at which the narrator will reach that BMI.

Because this poem is a dramatic monologue, we can expect it to reveal aspects of the narrator's psyche which she does not intend to divulge. We find here a complex and dysfunctional relationship in which her male partner encourages her to eat more and more, until – grotesquely – she rolls on top of him and he suffocates. This sudden end to their relationship appears not to be a source of great sorrow to the narrator, but she does not seem to feel liberated either.

In some cultures, and in some historical eras, the ideal of female beauty has been fat, because fatness can be associated in some ways with fertility. Currently, in our culture, debate continues about the use in advertising and fashion of so-called "size zero" models; many people are uncomfortable with the potential for impressionable young people to see unnaturally thin models as an ideal to emulate, with potential dangers to their own physical and mental health.

Feminists have long been concerned with the idea that women go to great lengths to please men, so that they are disempowered from choosing what to wear, how to look, or behave. Carol Ann Duffy's poem "Thetis" addresses this issue powerfully and with flair. It is among a very entertaining and thought-provoking collection of her poems, "The World's Wife" (1999).

The narrator in Agbabi's poem does what she is told to do; her partner derives pleasure from seeing her becoming fatter and fatter, while her pleasure is much more constricted ("my only pleasure the rush of fast food", which has no taste and brings no lasting satisfaction). The wobbly rhyme of **judder** and **juggernaut** is amusing in a slightly grisly way, and the metaphor "I was his Jacuzzi" is evocative- she is warm and wet and utterly shapeless, or circular.

The first five stanzas all end with full stops, and, up to this point, the narrator is in control of the narrative, which is largely objective and factual. It is from stanza five onwards that her feelings begin to emerge, via descriptive language.

Without shame, but with what we perceive as growing distress, she describes herself as a beached whale and a tidal wave of flesh, before the plaintive refrain "too fat" appears in stanza seven. A desert island and a whale are solid objects; a tidal wave is liquid (though perhaps semi – solid). Stanzas seven and eight feature milk (liquid), olive oil (liquid), and flowing flesh (liquid).

The nautical language continues, with the repeated rolling and drowning in stanza 9. The whole situation is indeed a "shipwreck", and the graphic description of him dead in the penultimate line makes him, too, look like a drowned man or a landed fish.

The phrase in stanza 3 "get up and walk round the bed" reminds me of the Biblical parable in St John's Gospel, chapter 5, in the New Testament. There, Jesus cures a disabled man who cannot reach the healing waters; he has been unable to walk for **thirty-eight** years. Note that our narrator will "hit **thirty-nine**" in stanza eight. Jesus tells the man "Rise, take up thy bed, and walk", and the man experiences a miraculous cure. In the same way, this poem presents a miraculous escape from infirmity for the narrator, who, we may suppose, is also thirty-eight- precisely the same age as the man Jesus rescues and heals!

It is instructive to compare this poem with Sue Boyle's "A Leisure Centre is Also a Temple of Learning". Both poems explore notions of female beauty and attraction, but in entirely different ways.

This poem comes to an end with three one-liners- or sentences which take up one line each. Six hours is perhaps the interval between main mealtimes. His "greed" for satiating his own appetite (for girls, girls, girls, in stanza four, with masses of cellulite) has become fatal. The last line leaves open the possibility that, in compliance with the words of the title of the poem, the narrator now eats him!

In Lewis Carroll's book, "Alice in Wonderland", Alice finds a cake, with the words "Eat me" inscribed on it, in currants. When she eats it, she grows, and describes herself as "opening out like the largest telescope that ever was". The intertextual reference suggests that the poem is a fantasy story; not to be taken too literally; and, in Alice's case, swelling to a plus size (in height) is temporary and reversible.

In the poem, however, the narrator's partner simply encourages her to keep eating; to go on from a BMI of 30 to 39, and he anticipates 40 with pleasure. This can only be unhealthy. Nobody should compromise their health like this; particularly not if they are tempted to do so because of pressure from others.

Simon Armitage   Chainsaw versus the Pampas Grass

Armitage often writes poems in the voice of unbalanced people who have a secret or shameful taste for violence. In this poem, the owner of the chainsaw identifies closely with it. Because the chainsaw is personified, and the user of it describes its actions as his own (I...carved at the trunk), the chainsaw becomes an extension of him, and they are hard to distinguish from each other.

The chainsaw starts and finishes the poem hanging from a hook in an underground dungeon or cellar. In this dark room, it grinds its teeth and it seethes with anger. This defining quality of anger is developed in the third stanza (instant rage/ lashing out/ bloody desire/flare).

It goes beyond what we can relate to as being reasonable or proportionate. It has a "grand plan" to satisfy its "sweet tooth" for skin and bones; it is primitive and sinister, like Ted Hughes' hawk which tears off the heads of its prey in "Hawk Roosting". Rather like Hughes' hawk, the chainsaw has become arrogant about its powerful superiority, so that, in the title of the poem, it is not "the chainsaw" but just "Chainsaw"- as though it were a superhero like Batman or Superman.

The confrontation between it and the pampas grass is likely to be a massacre (an unlikely match/ the sledgehammer taken to crack the nut). The chainsaw devours engine oil, bones, flesh and brains if and whenever it can- its appetite is insatiable. The second stanza contrasts its helpless state when unplugged with its destructive potential when it is connected to an electric socket. It is like an automatic or machine gun, and the extension lead is like a trail of gunpowder waiting to be lit.

The pampas grass has the fourth stanza to itself. It is sunbathing among a variety of soft furnishings, blissfully unaware of what is about to attack it. Its twelve-foot spears will be no match for its electrical executioner. The grass is fragile and feminine; it swoons when the chainsaw touches it.

Until the fifth stanza, all the narrator has done is to oil and plug the chainsaw in. Now, he is seduced by its power- "this was a game….overkill". It is not the chainsaw which rips and carves- it is him. Ripping into "pockets of dark, secret warmth" seems improper, a violation- almost an act of rape.

The narrator goes on, in stanza 6, methodically clearing the battleground of the garden of casualties, and the poem uses the military language of gunfire and swordplay- raked/severed/felled/ torn/ dead/ fired/ cut/ drove/ blade/ sliced/ split/ cutting/ knife. Armitage's poem shares the concept of the garden as a battlefield with Vernon Scannell's "Nettles", in which the narrator, who feels guilty about his son's nettle stings, scythes and burns the nettles, only for them to grow back. The pampas grass grows back too, in defiance of the way it has been felled, while defenceless.

The point of Scannell's poem is that, as parents, we want to protect our children from harm, but we cannot (and nor should we try to).

Armitage's poem works on the level of seeing gardening as an outlet for an instinct to be violent. If it has a deeper meaning, I suggest that it is observing that violence- perhaps terrorism- creates devastation in the short term, but societies- in the same way as the pampas grass- find ways of reasserting themselves, slowly, so that the triumph and disruption of outrageous violence is outlasted by the gentler virtues of the non-violent.

In growing back, even grander than before, the pampas grass is a symbol of life. "Corn in Egypt" is a quotation from the Old Testament (Genesis, chapter 42); having corn in Egypt is the key to surviving hostile times, of drought or conflict. The alliterative oxymoron "midday moon" suggests that the destruction of the pampas grass, and its need to be restored, is an aberration from the natural order of things, because the moon is visible at midnight; or that, as the moon looks weak and pale by daylight, the narrator's violence is made impotent by the regrowth of the pampas grass.

The poem ends with the point that the chainsaw's murderous dreams are "man-made"; they are fuelled by, and originate in, the narrator, because he is alive, while the chainsaw is merely an object personified. The narrator is desentisized to the environmental impact of his own addiction to unjustified violence, but the natural world is not, and the natural world reasserts the natural order- a concept we are familiar with from Shakespeare's tragedies.

Ros Barber   Material

The poem has 9 stanzas. Each stanza has 8 lines, except for stanza 6, which has 9. In each stanza, the last line rhymes with the one two lines earlier (slab/crab, tears/dears etc). Lines 2 and 4 of each stanza also rhyme most of the time. The rhyme pattern implies a desire to hold on to the past, and to the simplicity and regularity of childhood, but the solid rhyme- the life of the 1960s- cannot be sustained rigidly, just as the "material" handkerchief has been replaced by a disposable paper tissue.

This poem (like "Effects") sets down a narrator's memories of their dead mother; but this one also includes memories of the narrator's childhood- buying from the greengrocer/butcher/fishmonger in stanza 5; dancing lessons in stanza 6; old money and home baking in stanza 7.

Also as with "Effects", the single word which gives the poem its title has a dual meaning. Here, "material" denotes both the fabric of the handkerchief and the stuff out of which the narrator's life and attitudes as a parent have been formed.

Stanzas 1-4 and 7-9 explore the mother's attitude to "hankies", and the daughter's.

The narrator still feels tied emotionally to her mother, and the use of the symbol of the handkerchief makes this more concrete. The (childish) words hanky/hankies occur ten times in the first 8 stanzas; then there is the more formal "handkerchiefs" twice. The narrator concedes that "Nostalgia only makes me old"- looking back is enervating and it induces "lassitude".

The narrator mentions that her mother was scrupulous in using the lace handkerchief to keep her own children's faces clean (stanza 2); she herself has "neglected-looking kids, the kind whose noses strangers clean". Paper tissues feature in stanzas 1, 8 and 9. The contrast between their cheap disposable character and the "material" (cloth/lace) of the traditional hanky reinforces the material in the poem about the changing face of shopping- malls and late-night garages and shops, and how they have replaced the department/family stores, and mobile shops in the form of "a Comma van".

The cloth "material" is solid, and it brings with it memories which it is easy to visualise and to relate in a poem. It is a symbol of the "old" way of life of the 1960s. The generation which used the old clothes and methods (stanza 4) has "died", so that the hanky itself is a symbol of "loss" (stanza 5) and "history". It was used, in the past, to regulate emotion- grief in stanza 1 and tears in stanza 6.

Sean O'Brien's poem in this collection uses the mining tradition, and its dying out, to connect the past with the present in a very similar way.

Barber's narrator speaks of her "awkwardness" in not carrying tissues, and her mother's "embarrassment" in never going without a hanky, and stanza 7 associates the messiness and loss of innocence of "my brood" with the television age and "bought biscuits".

Mothers are always on the point of feeling awkward about their skills with their own children; in this case, the nose-blowing or child-cleaning item has changed with the times, but having one with you at all times is a priority for one generation; the younger generation learns to live with social embarrassment and to brush it aside, as something which does not define you.

The want of a handkerchief would define the narrator, in her own mind, as inadequate, just as O'Brien's miners defined themselves by the lack of the things they did not have.

A group of words- grief/ loss/ died/ tears/killed/ let it go/ died- reminds us that this poem features a dead relative, and the language in the final stanza echoes the world of wills (leaving.....what you will). Even the narrator's mother "eventually" used disposable tissues; they are presented to us as symbolising a more laissez-faire approach to life. The narrator's mother had let her own child go and had let the hanky go; the narrator will, in time, have to do the same; live in the present and let her own memories of her own childhood go.

The final three stanzas of the poem focus less on the handkerchiefs and more on the narrator's self-assessment as a parent. She only has time to write the poem because she has turned the television on and put her children in front of it. Buying this time for herself is paid for in the loss of her children's innocence. She accuses herself of inadequacy, because she won't "commit to being home". Towards the end of stanza 8, "I miss material handkerchiefs" really means "I miss my mother".

The difficulty in adjusting your relationship with a dead parent is a theme this poem shares with those by Jenkins and Thorpe.

Eavan Boland　　　　　**Inheritance**

Here we have a mother thinking about what she has, which she can, or should, pass on to her children. Eavan Boland is a female Irish poet who has observed that Ireland is one of few countries with a Constitution which defines the role of women as homemaking or domestic.

The poem presents us with a peculiarly female and Irish dilemma- this woman has no material possessions, no jewellery or silk clothing, because, in this country, there is poverty ("want") and women of earlier generations had only the craft of knitting, which cannot be inherited. It can only be learned.

The "inland distances" are inward-looking, the island (of Ireland) "of waters"; there is no prospect for women here of the international travel and independence of the map woman.

The narrator presents hers as a family without heirlooms; as she has no commercial skills or knowledge, all she can pass on is her observations about the world- not a view (which she does not own), but the instinct to care for your own children and believe in their resilience.

The first three stanzas define the limitations she faces. She can show her daughters a view, but she does not "really" own the ground she stands on to see it. Heirlooms like jewellery do not exist in her family.

Stanza 4 is a statement of the position of women in Ireland; women are not the owners of anything, and so, having nothing, they cannot create something to leave behind- except, of course, their children.

Line 13 begins with a jokey surprise; we expect it to say "I learned so much from them", but it says "so little". As King Lear says in Shakespeare's tragedy, "nothing will come of nothing".

Similarly, in line 17, the crafts of spinning and knitting- which would have tied her to repeat the subservience and domestic servitude of previous generations of women- "are all crafts I never had"; so, there again, there is nothing to pass on. Half way though line 18, the tone changes, with the antithetical sentence starting with "But"; here, at last, is the essential legacy. It is the ability to reassure your child, when they are ill or in distress; perhaps even the skill of pretending to know "the secrets of health and air", even when you don't.

We have fever and then "the absence of fever"; nothing and then something; the crafts I never had and the ability to calm a child which "I must have learned....somewhere".

If we apply the helpful dogma that the meaning of a poem is often to be found in its final word, this poem is about "somewhere"- a place where women, like this narrator, have the possibility of escaping to. While having nothing in the way of valuable possessions, they can learn something and pass it on to their daughters- education, perhaps, or a life outside the home, or economic independence.

The local view is "no good". That is the physical view in stanza 2, but it is also the cultural view which Ireland itself has of its women; that they have no right to escape poverty. The idea that women should be "barefoot and pregnant" is one we regard as almost medieval.

Three Rock Mountain is outside Dublin; it is important as a landmark which enables broadcasters to transmit to their audiences. It does not seem to have the power to transmit important ideas about freedom or the wider world to the narrator and her daughters.

The final four lines of the poem universalise the narrator's experience. Although the environment in Ireland is so unsupportive of aspiration for women, she has learned how to nurse a child. That competence seems to be independent of the setting. It is not because she is in Ireland that she has absorbed it; it is because she is a mother.

The phrase "leave behind" can refer to a bequest or inheritance for others; but the narrator may also be expressing the feeling that she needs to leave this Ireland behind. The drive to achieve "something......somewhere" is dragged down by the threat of "never/not ever/never/never/nothing/never" The land of never is not neverneverland. Ireland is presented here as a land of tears, water, and the oppression of women. If the choice for the next generation of women is the same, then "somewhere"-anywhere- is preferable to this.

The need to leave (and the need to arrive) recurs in the poems by Doshi and Duffy in particular, but also with Flynn and Nagra.

Sue Boyle A Leisure Centre is also a Temple of Learning

This poem focuses on a girl who is getting changed after swimming in a leisure centre pool. She is beautifying herself, consciously and assiduously, making herself so attractive that (like nectar) a bee could sip her.

The poem emphasises how young she is- a girl in the women's changing room/ a young leopard/ so much younger- and that she has natural advantages; perfect bone structure and natural beauty. She is merely "making her body more beautiful" than it already is. Is a young leopard prey or predator? In preparing herself to attract a bee (an insect with a sting, which consumes pollen), and in adopting the sweet colour of honey and the smoothness of cream, she is turning herself into an object of attraction, an exhibit. She uses an aromatic scrub and a gentle exfoliant, moisturiser and perfume. It is the perfume of a flower which attracts the bee to sip it.

The girl's face is not described. The focus is on erogenous parts of her body (hands, throat, ears, underchin, hair, breasts, thighs) and the most intimate areas- "her secret cleft is shaved". She pays microscopic attention to "every part that might be loved". Note the precise focus- not on her ears and breasts but specifically on "the little kisspoints below" and "the nuzzle between".

She does all this, absorbed in a state of dreamy abstractedness, unaware that she is a natural prey, and that she is making herself even more appealing, and even more likely to be preyed upon, by accentuating her attractiveness with these artificial aids.

The sense that she may, perhaps subconsciously, be willing to be objectified- or even want to do that to herself- is reminiscent of Agbabi's "Eat Me". One possible reading of both poems will find the two women- for all their physical differences- wanting to be admired, and becoming exhibitionist.

Because she is young, she does not know what the chorus (the group of older women) knows- its experience, wittily, makes the leisure centre "a temple of learning".

In Greek drama (and in Shakespeare's "Romeo and Juliet") the chorus knows in advance what will happen next. Perhaps, here, it knows that the young leopard will go out to play and hunt, and will also be hunted itself; that the real world outside the temple (a place where we worship beauty for its own sake, rather than in a sexual way- see Keats' Ode on a Grecian Urn, and the way Tim Turnbull reshapes this in his poem) is rough and dangerous, less genteel and protected than the changing room; in reality, wild, and sometimes cruel.

Older women know that physical beauty fades; that self-absorption is a poor basis for lasting relationships; that this young girl has much growing up to do, much "learning" to acquire.

The poem has no men in it. Yet the girl is turning herself into a sexual object- not consciously, but "in dreamy abstractedness"- and the poetic language- four similes and the powerful metaphor "she is summer cream slipped over raspberries" – cannot dissipate a rather voyeuristic tone. This is the difference between the observers, who know, and the subject of the poem, who does not even know that she is being watched or observed.

The older women, Sue Boyle has said, want to protect this girl – a girl who is inviting sexual intimacy without really being aware of the complications it involves, or being properly prepared for it.

John Burnside   History

This long, 73-line poem is written in the wake of the Al Qaeda attack which destroyed the twin towers of the World Trade Center in New York on 11 September 2001. Two hijacked passenger jets were flown into the buildings, which collapsed, killing hundreds of people who were trapped inside the offices in the towers, or jumped from them to their deaths.

This event prompts the narrator's uneasy mood (lines 12-14). "That gasoline smell" may be a reference to a gasoline smell at the scene of the murderous attack in New York, and the war planes (lines 10-11) may be a show of defence. The references to **property** and **gravity** in lines 30-31 remind us of the towers' collapse, and the **virtual trade** in line 43 alludes to the financial focus in those offices, where people were "captive.....slow-burning" (lines 54-57).

While the first 22 lines are a narrative- an account of the speaker's time on the beach with his son, a toddler- the remainder of the poem (a dramatic monologue) ruminates on the possible consequences of "the irredeemable", as the closing clause emphatically puts it.

The narrator fears some cataclysm in which the world we know is destroyed (lines 40-42), presumably through a nuclear war. He defines "the problem" as how to live your life "and do no harm"- how to avoid giving offence to someone who will react as terrorists do.

His instinct tells him (lines 23-29) that our family ties, our cultural heritage, and our nationality are of no real importance, or at least that they should not define us to the rest of the world, because there is something much greater than this- a common heritage. As citizens of the world, we should, regardless of nationality and culture, be able to share dreams. He feels that when we lose that wider sense of global citizenship, "the irredeemable" follows- some action which will lead to irreversible consequences. This is the danger if we respond to an outrage with a defensive, territorial retreat into the bunker of our own nationalism.

Therefore, the poem suggests, whoever we are, and wherever we are- in the USA, or on an east-facing beach in Scotland, or wherever else- we cannot escape whatever will follow from "what may come". The physical distance which separates us from 9/11 may muffle the "dread" of destruction on a world scale, but it cannot drive it away altogether.

Several parts of the poem are preoccupied with tiny pieces of marine life and the detritus of the seashore- lines 15-22, 32-37, 50-61,67-68.

As a parent, the speaker is simultaneously "afraid, attentive, patient"; apprehensive that the world his young son is growing up in will be destroyed by the consequences of that day's "irredeemable" events i.e. the retaliation and escalation of an East-West conflict driven by ideology.

While he, the father, is puzzled and worried by the philosophical and political implications, the small boy is "puzzled by the pattern on a shell".

What washes up on the coast of East Scotland has come from other parts of the globe, and possibly other oceans; shells and pebbles, smudges of weed and flesh, fish lodged in the tide, wood and dried weed. While this absorbs the child, his parents are flying kites, "plugged into the sky/ all nerve and line".

The reference to kites and to plugs alludes to another presence in the background of this poem- that of Benjamin Franklin (1706-90). Franklin is sometimes called "the first American". As one of its founding fathers, he signed both the Declaration of Independence and the American Constitution; he was America's first ambassador to France.

He was also a scientist; he used a kite in a storm to show that lightning was an electrical charge, and he invented the lightning rod (is this relevant to the "shifts of light and weather" in lines 46-47?). Throughout his life, Franklin was a great advocate of religious pluralism and tolerance.

Franklin stands behind the poem as a symbol of how the USA could- and perhaps should- respond to 9/11- not with anger and retribution, but with virtue; seeking to build a tolerant consensus rather than a conflict based on religious or cultural dogma. Franklin himself belonged to no religious group, but he was a Deist- he thought that the divine could be detected in the world around us. It follows from this that no religion has a monopoly on God or on doctrine. This seems to me to chime with the internationalist and almost pantheistic sentiments in the poem, particularly in lines 23-39.

Running parallel with this strand of thought is the interestingly detailed catalogue of fish in the poem. Some of them are very young (spawn) and others are of indeterminate age, or dead (shreds of razorfish/jellyfish/ sea anemone/the fish/carp/sticklebacks/ goldfish). None of them "do harm"; they are diverse, but share the common ground that they are all fish, wherever they have come from.

The fish is a complex cultural symbol; of Christian sacrifice, of the subconscious, of bad news and disaster, and of the exotic and invisible depths of the world under the sea. All of Burnside's fish are here because their movements are governed by something fluid, which crosses national boundaries- "the book of silt and tides". Adults are "tethered .....to gravity and light" through our communality with these fish; like them, we should swim with the tide and go wherever it takes us, but as separately identifiable types of fish. We cannot rise above "our given states" because, unlike the kites, we are "fixed and anchored to the shore" in our physical bodies; what we can do, however, is to "register the drift and tug of other bodies", and - like a toddler- "apprehend the moment as it happens".

Some of the poems in the Edexcel selection have a strong sense of a national character or temperament, whether it is English (Barber, Duffy, Fanthorpe) or Indian (Padel, Nagra). Burnside seems to avoid any strong sense of Scottishness here; the golf links possibly "links" this beach with other beaches in all other parts of the world, and this golf course with the golf courses of the USA (golf is a popular sport in Scotland and the USA).

There is a small selection of words which appear more than once in the poem- today/ distance/ light/ world/beach/ shells/ scarcely/ tides. None of them is specific to a location; the tide is far out. It is "in water" (which covers most of the Earth's surface) that we find our connectivity, and escape the anchors of "our given states"- the nationalism, cultural or religious, which makes us "irredeemable", or incapable of being saved.

Lastly, **the twin towers were a pair of buildings; this poem is full of pairings**- Lucas/Leuchars, far out and quail-grey, cambered and turned, mind and dread, shells and pebbles, weed and flesh, own and dream, fixed and anchored, gravity and light, distance and the shapes, silt and tides, rose or petrol blue, jellyfish and sea anemone, drift and tug, light and weather, captive and bright, spawn and stickleback, gazed-upon and cherished, wood and dried weed, nerve and line.

We could, perhaps, add "chalk and cheese" or "salt and pepper" or "black and white". The twin towers stood together and fell together (or, as Benjamin Franklin had said, at the signing of the American Declaration of Independence, " We must, indeed, all hang together, or most assuredly we shall all hang separately"). World peace- avoiding the holocaust of lines 41-42- depends not on the internal solidarity of individual nations, but on the solidarity of the global, supranational community of nations.

Ciaran Carson   The War Correspondent

(the sections 1 Gallipoli and 4 Balaklava are studied, and as two separate poems)

Carson (born in Belfast, 1948) is interested in the potential of language and words. He has been interested, too, in the reports of WH Russell to The Times newspaper from the Crimean War. In the absence of documentary film, or Instagram, such reports were all the domestic public had to rely upon; but they must, by definition, be selective in their detail and their representation.

Just as a painting of a battle scene will depict it from an editorial point of view- and that will depend on who is paying for the painting, and who is painting it- a written account of a war, or episodes from it, will be selective. Wilfred Owen intended his poems, in the First World War, to give a **realistic** account of life and death in the front line, as opposed to the **propaganda** which appeared in the newspapers to reassure domestic readers that the War was going well.

The two episodes here- "Gallipoli" and "Balaklava"- do not feature fighting at all. "Gallipoli" is a poem of ten stanzas, each five lines long. It builds a kaleidoscope of detail, colours and smells. The town is a chaos of its usual inhabitants and combatants, and the two categories are mixed in together- employers, riflemen, Zouaves, camel-drivers, officers, sailors, sappers, miners, slaves, money-changers , interpreters, tailors, troops, opium-smokers, spies, whores and soldiers.

These occupations are not the only list. The sixth stanza lists eleven types of clothing. Thirteen different nationalities or allegiances are listed. There are twelve place names (Billingsgate, Dublin, Benares, Boulogne, Sheffield, Bologna, Springfield, Valenciennes, Byzantine, Kimberley, Trebizond, Gallopoli), and twenty-seven objects, mainly to do with the architecture of urban areas (tenements, slaughter-houses, stalls, sheds etc.).

There is a cluster of words to do with food- it is typically eclectic; cantaloupes, garlic, oregano, linguini, sherbet, lemonade, lard, wine, plums, apricots, brandy.

There are some smells and scents, all of them unpleasant- dung and straw, rotten meat, a stagnant harbour, sewers, offal, stench. Most significantly of all, the adjectives are almost all negative and unharmonious - failing, riddled, jangly, sour, temporary, tumbledown, ruinous, leaking, dirty, tainted, rotten, bad, rancid.

It is arresting that, at the end of stanza nine, when we have been caught up in all of this activity, the idea that the Allied "powers" are failing appears; and that it is discussed by "spies and whores", not by the military planners who should be aware of it.

This undercurrent of impending disaster is developed through **the language of disease**- cholera, swarming with flies; and **of death**- shrouds, dead or drunk, slaughter-houses. The local brandy is called "grape-shot"- which is also a term for a type of ammunition fired from cannons.

The form of the poem is, firstly, in eight stanzas which all open with an imperative (take….); it is almost like the recipe for a stew, or instructions to a painter (indeed , Andrew Marvell's poem from 1667, "The Last Instructions to a Painter", adopts the same approach, using imperatives to command the reader to pay attention, in a polite way).

Carson's small details add up to a detailed canvas, and the description of each scene is very visual. However, at the end of 50 lines, he declares that "I have not even begun to describe Gallipoli"; there is much more to be written, quite apart from the story of the military campaign itself, which lasted from April 1915 until January 1916, and in which, on both sides, in aggregate perhaps half a million men died.

The final two stanzas- which still form part of the single sentence the poem comprises, like the sweep of a wide-angle lens- invoke the landscape, and tell us that, even before the fighting starts, "soldiers lie dead" here. Alternatively, this could be the scene *after* the battle (as is the case with "Balaklava"), when the army and its transport is waiting to leave. Either way, we are conscious that the oriental way of life here will continue, regardless of any temporary, rude intrusions from Western Europe. Stanzas 1-4 encapsulate the arrivals of the English, the Irish, the French and the Italians, who are to be injected, in stanza 5, into "this slum", and dressed in the local style (stanza 6).

Read as a list of the resources needed to mount a military expedition, the poem seems chronically, and ironically, inadequate. As readers, we are asking ourselves how organisation can ever emerge from this melting pot of squalor. The multi-cultural mix is reflected in the complex linguistic origins, or etymology of words. Fezzes, for instance, are Turkish; oubliettes, French; linguini, Italian; you could investigate the etymology of the more exotic words for yourself.

There is a rhyme/ homophone scheme which couples stanzas in pairs. You can follow them until towards the end of the poem- gate/estate, fish/dish, yards/yards, horses/Benares, Dublin/tin; Boulogne/Bologna, meet/meat, Sheffield/Springfield, towers/employers, destroyers/Power's; Turk/needlework, riflemen/Valenciennes, sailors/tailors, lingo/flamingo and changers/stranger. Note, though, that, here, in stanzas 5 and 6, the last two lines are misplaced in terms of the rhyme. We would expect "flamingo" to end the stanza, as the ending of its fifth line, but it is the end of the fourth line instead.

The coupling of stanzas 7 and 8 is still consistent, but it varies the previous pattern; now, lines 2 and 3 rhyme within the same stanza, not with the corresponding lines in the next one.

The pattern of the rhymes in stanzas 9 and 10 is different again; Kimberley/Gallipoli (lines 1 and 5); Trebizond/ beyond (lines 2 and 1); rugs/ snugs and apricots/grape-shot in adjacent lines; powers/flowers (lines 5 and 4).

Rhyme is maintained, but it becomes progressively more difficult to do so. The weakening grip on the construction of the rhyme may, metaphorically, reflect the Allies' "failing prowess". We may also interpret it to mean that the use of rhyme to control such disorderly material as this poem contains is, in itself, like "the oubliettes of Trebizond"- dungeons, or box-like structures, hidden below the surface, and belonging to an earlier age. When you first read the poem, you may not have noticed that there is a rhyme scheme, because it is obscured by the richness and complexity of the poem's language.

4 Balaklava

Carson's interest in war reporting focuses particularly on the Crimean War. Balaklava was a battle in that war, fought on 25th October 1854; it featured the Charge of the Light Brigade, a disastrous cavalry attack based on a misunderstanding about the intended target.

Tennyson, the Poet Laureate, commemorated this event in his poem of the same name. His is an ambiguous and ambivalent poem which praises the hopeless heroism of the British soldiers, while it also laments the outcome, calling the location "the valley of Death", and confirming that "someone had blunder'd". The loss of life is accented. The operation is noble, but it is a failure, for readers who care to detect that undertone.

The issue of war reporting therefore concerns the need to be **accurate**, or as **fair-minded** as your commission and your readers will permit you to be. There is also the issue of **how you write** a war report. It is easy to be jingoistic and/or to be carried away by a sense of patriotism, but wars are about ending lives prematurely; this demands and deserves a serious and balanced approach.

"Balaklava" (adopting the Turkish spelling of the place-name) is a poem in four stanzas of eight lines. Each line in stanza 1 rhymes with the matching line in stanza 2- steel/cochineal etc; there is a small variation in the final lines, in that **floor** and **flora** are very similar, but they do not strictly rhyme.

The same pattern governs stanzas 3 and 4, but with one exception. Green/clean and mounds/wolfhound adhere to the pattern. But **bones** and **repose** do not rhyme. Then shoots/boots, day/lay, horseman/rataplan, arms/arms, and jacket/jackets either rhyme or repeat each other (these last two repetitions imply the repetitive pattern of armies fighting, with predictably fatal results).

What, then, are we to make of the exception- repose and bones? Perhaps it exists, striking a discordant and uncomfortable note, to highlight that **repose**- like "falling" in battle- is a **euphemism** for death, and an unsatisfactory one.

We might expect a poem called "Balaklava" to describe the battle there; but, just as "Gallipoli" does not, it does not. It observes the march of the Turkish army after the battle- in fact, **some time afterwards**, since the skeletons of the dead have been picked clean. The flowers and colours in the first two stanzas are poetic DNA which relates and connects this poem to "Gallipoli".

The narrative here is overtly subjective- as the similes, the impressionistic phrase "caught the eye", and the selection of detail (colours on uniforms, itemising the flora) all concede.

Stanzas 3 and 4 are different; they stop treating military matters as an artistic endeavour. The language of death starts to feature in stanza 3- slain/ deadly/fatal/ skeleton/ buttons/ jacket.

Lines 22-28, inserted into the middle of a stanza without warning, are shocking and disturbing. The English horseman is one of the dead cavalrymen of the Light Brigade. The buttons have been taken as a trophy, and the shallow graves have been ineffectual; the dead have had their boots taken by the living. We talk about bravery being "dying with your boots on"; these men did that, but their boots- the sign of their bravery- were taken from them by their killers. Their courage has no witnesses to celebrate it. They are mere skeletons now.

To describe a dead soldier as a skeleton, and then to focus on the small details in lines 25-27, is the antithesis of the "heroic" style of reporting; it is brutally realistic. Even today, we have a reporting convention that dead bodies are not shown on TV news, although other forms of media do not have the same rules to govern them.

While there is a certain pathos to lines 22-28, the final four lines of the poem disturb us with their language of rot and decay. There is no time to stop and reflect or mourn; the rataplan, a drumroll, induces the marchers to "sweep on". Notably, the narrator now sees himself as one of them; they are "we", not "The

Turks". The view in line 5 is from a distance, but in line 31 the narrator is in the midst of the marchers.

The buttoned-up jackets are, of course, jackets with buttons on them (unlike the jackets of the dead). However, the adjective "buttoned-up" also denotes an emotional detachment or constriction, and this war reporter does not or will not stop to reflect on the carnage and pathos of these deaths. He "sweeps on over" the bodies of the dead instead- perhaps not realising that the jacketed and buttoned-up marcher of today is the jacketed, buttonless corpse of tomorrow.

The language of the poem emphasises four loci of meaning- the flora, meadows, grass and flowers; the armaments (steel/barrels/firelocks/bayonets/shot/bullet-skull/ bristling/flashed/ powder); the uniforms and the marching (boots/ jackets/polished/infantry/ advanced/ phalanxes/ buttons/ columns/uniforms); and **death** (crushed/ fallen/smothered/ cut off/ slain/ deadly/ fatal/ skeleton/ hanging/ bones/ shot/ mounds/ graves/black/ red/scarlet/ poppies/ plucked/ soil).

As with "Gallipoli", the narrator protests his incompetence to itemise everything adequately ("countless other plants whose names I lack"). This implies that he finds it difficult to be selective over detail. The reading experience contradicts this- the imagery is photographic in character, and it tells us all we need to know.

In both poems, Carson shows us the potential language has to represent the events in and surrounding armed conflict in an orderly or disorderly way. Through the positioning of the narrator, he asks us to consider the difficulties of reporting objectively in such a febrile and dangerous environment. Reporters or correspondents make judgments, form impressions, and sometimes do not have the time, or do not choose to make the time, to reflect properly on what they see. This means that they are not necessarily reliable. **War reporting – like war itself- is a battlefield**, in which the wrong words can be deployed; misunderstandings are commonplace. Objectivity is very difficult to maintain.

These poems for Edexcel generally present the narrator as non-intrusive; narrators facilitate the point the poet wants to make. The narrator in Motion's poem is the other great interventionist in the collection.

Julia Copus   An Easy Passage

This poem seems straightforward, but the language is subtle and the meaning is opaque.

The poem is like a photograph. It captures a moment when a thirteen-year-old girl climbs through an upstairs window into her home- although, instead of the word "home", the less intimate phrase "her family's house" is used.

The house is "set back from the street", but the child can still be observed by a secretary in the factory over the road- a superstitious woman whose age is not specified, but whose life seems to be unambitious.

Thirteen is the age of Juliet in Shakespeare's "Romeo and Juliet", and the number thirteen is thought to be unlucky in some countries and cultures. Wearing a silver anklet may perhaps be associated with warding off evil spirits; the girl's mother will not let her have a key (much like Juliet's mother); she looks down from the porch roof at the friend "with whom she is half in love" (like Juliet in the so-called balcony scene). The references to astrology (which we call, conversationally, "the stars"), and to "omens", remind us that the fate of the star-crossed Romeo and Juliet is written in the stars. Romeo and Juliet die just as they are starting to grow towards adulthood, and, at the core of this poem, there is a similar uncertainty- though no tragic undertone- about the thirteen-year-old's future course in life.

For now, she concentrates intently on the need to "keep her mind" on the task of getting into the house though the window. We are used, nowadays, to the casual use of the word *window* to mean *opportunity*; her opportunity still lies within her family, at least for the time being.

While the "flush-faced secretary" is indoors, on a hot day, the two girls have been sunbathing (bikini/warm/hot beneath her toes/beach) - not on a real beach, but in this suburban setting. While the child/girl dares to overcome the obstacle of lacking a key to get back into the house, and spends time with her friend, the secretary dreams absently of evening classes and travel, but there is no sign that she will do either of them in the foreseeable future. She appears to be fatalistic, instead of keeping her mind on the present; she leaves the future to fate, to omens and the horoscopes in whatever she reads. This passive approach to life would probably seem alien and even pathetic to the vast majority of thirteen-year-olds.

The child is "halfway up", and "half in love"; is the age of 13 halfway to adulthood? While the environment of the observer (the secretary) is drab, the two young girls, and their world, are associated with **the language of light**- blond gravel/ lightly/ seem lit/ gold/ silver/ shimmering-oyster-painted/ sunlight/ flash.

There is a distinction between photographic, or literal, and imaginative reality in the poem. The house is solid and physical- porch roof/windowsill/ stairwell/ open window/ aluminium lever/ house/ house/ driveway/ house. The two teenage children are solid too, with their eyes/fingertips/tiny breasts/ thighs/ hair/ earrings/ ears/ calf/ toenails/ foot/whole body, but they are delicate and fragile, though adventurous.

We are not told why the girl's mother will not trust her with a key, but it seems likely that she wants to keep her as a small, dependent child for as long as possible. The repetition of the word *far* shows that, for the thirteen-year-old, a different vision is emerging. It is as if the mother is holding on to her child by the fingertips; her daughter is petrified of falling, when she tries to get back inside the house.

The poem uses two similes. The girls "seem lit, as if from within"; the secretary does not- her "flush face" is not so luminous! Nor is the secretary in the sunlight. Even if she, too, has painted toe-nails, they do not catch the light "like armaments"- exotic, dangerous, powerful things.

The children's positive attitude and resourcefulness is threatened by the rhetorical question at the heart of the poem (lines 17-19), which couples growing (in age, and the desire for independence) with non-admittance to what we hope for ourselves; the secretary is the embodiment of that loss of energy and self-determination, because secretaries are at the beck and call of those they work for.

The rhetorical question is framed by two long sentences; lines 1-13 are one sentence (about a thirteen-year-old!), and lines 19-39 also form a single sentence, which encompasses the two girls, the secretary who sees them, and the disappearance of the girl into "her family's house". The house is warm, but it is only a home in a flimsy, unhomely sense, and it offers shade; the wider world is hot, and far away, and a place where life is a beach.

Julia Copus believes in something we might call the revolving door theory; that what we become, and the course of our lives, is determined by apparently accidental or random choices we make.

If that theory applies here, the thirteen-year-old, in returning to the keyless and mistrustful "family's house", may be allowing her desire for freedom and adventure to be reined in, at least for the time being. Perhaps she is not yet equipped to become a Juliet, a self-determiner, without enacting Juliet's tragic fate.

If growing up is, then, a process of compromise, as we find that "the world admits us less and less", does the same life as the secretary's await her? Or can she still carve out a different path to some adult beach?

Tishani Doshi   The Deliverer

This unsettling poem has a primitive quality to it, despite its contemporary setting. Rather like Robert Minhinnick's fox in the museum, it asks us to consider what civilisation is, and how narrowly we are separated from and insulated against the most primitive and inhumane actions. The infanticide at the end of the poem is as barbaric as the slaughter of the mermaid in Roderick Ford's "Giuseppe"; in both cases, we ask ourselves whether this type of murder is in any sense morally excusable.

Milwaukee Airport is a relatively small airport, which does not receive flights from India direct. Kerala is a state in the south west of India. It has a very high proportion of female to male residents; education, jobs and skills for women are higher there than in any other part of India. It is, therefore, a region in which baby girls are not rejected as inferior to boys.

Infanticide is illegal in India (naturally!) but it still occurs, more so in rural communities; the expense of finding a dowry for a female child is problematic for poor families. This poem presents the murder of children as a consequence, not of poverty, but of the lack of contraception- and of the wider oppression/submissiveness of women (a reminder of Patience Agbabi's "Eat Me").

The characters in the poem - mother/sister/children/girls/parents/women/girl- are almost all female. Men are only mentioned once, as an afterthought, in the penultimate word of the poem. Meaning is often detectable particularly in the final words of a poem- in this case, those final words are "men again". Men, it seems, are a problem, and they are in no sense a part of the solution.

The identity of the narrator is held back. We know that her mother has gone to Kerala to adopt a child, and the immediacy of the conversation is achieved by the use of the present tense. The chosen child is the most damaged one, whose own mother had tried to bury her (lines 8, 16). The phrase "will bring" implies that the narrator is not present on this visit.

The second section of the poem contrasts the tradition or custom of infanticide with the American attitude to "ceremony and tradition", or doing the right thing. "The parents" suggests that the narrator's father, as well as her mother, is waiting, although we might expect "my parents".

The third of these three stanzas implies that "my mother" has lost a child. The second stanza in this section tells us that the full horror of the child's treatment by her mother has not been disclosed to the adoptive parents, and that "the baby" is unfamiliar with touch and is damaged psychologically. This child has been chosen, unseen, purely on the basis of the story the nun had told in stanza 2 of the first section of the poem.

The third section connects with the separate line 10 ("the one", "this girl"). The "twilight corners" are dim, obscure memories. The phrase "she's passed" is interesting; does it mean that she was passed, once and once only, from the nun to her adoptive mother; or that she is passed repeatedly from one adult woman to another once she is in America, because no-one will look after her permanently?

The final eight lines deal with these memories and the circumstances of infanticide. Women are continually pregnant , and if the child is not a boy it is thrown away. This sense of being abandoned or disowned is all there is, as the girl grows up; such a memory can't be dislodged. The language of the poem and its imagery are both brutal and sad- crippled/garbage/ stuffed/ abandoned/ dug/ chew/ plucking/bury/ empty/desolate/ squeeze out life/ toss the baby to the heap/ trudge.

The poem presents the idea that mothers both save and harm their children. The deliverer of the title is the nun, and/or "my mother", and/ or "her mother", and/or the women the girl is passed from and to.

The deliberate technique here, of disturbing or unsettling the reader, by not giving the characters who populate a poem more than a shadowy identity, is reminiscent of TS Eliot.

Unlike the individual characters, the images in the poem are well defined, and shocking- babies tossed in piles, or buried alive, or thrown out with the rubbish, because they are perceived as defective, by virtue of being the "wrong" gender; parents or adoptive parents crying at the airport as they await the arrival of children with fetishes and dark histories; and the primitive, ritualistic cycle, on the edge of society, of repeated childbirth and rejection.

The poem starts and ends with a matter-of-fact observation of the world as it is. The poem, like the mothers, does not object or rebel. While a fraction of these rejected children can be delivered to apparent safety, the quality of their lives (in America) is questionable. The underlying problem has not been resolved.

The poem is open to readings other than this humanitarian one. The use of America as a destination, and the exaggerated cultural differences of adopting there, may point to ideas about the usefulness of international aid.

We could see the poem as critical of western democracies' tendency to assume an attitude of moral superiority. Moreover, degrees of distress are not necessarily the only criterion on which aid should be prioritised.

A feminist reading will see the poem as a statement about the lack of self-determination which women experience, in at least some parts of the world, even today. This would make the choice of Kerala especially provocative, as it is the part of India where the experience of women is the most unlike what the poem describes.

Carol Ann Duffy   The Map Woman

This is a long narrative poem in 13 stanzas of 10 lines each.

The conceit of someone's body being a map derives from John Donne's "Hymne to God my God, in my sicknesse", written in 1631. The idea in Duffy's poem is that we eventually outgrow the ties to our childhood which come to be less relevant as we grow older and more independent. Just as Donne's idea was original, Duffy takes it further by relating the process of reaching maturity as being complete when, like a snake, you shed your childhood skin.

The town is Stafford, where she grew up from the age of six. It is therefore reasonable to suppose that the map woman is Duffy herself. Using her own memories is a common part of her method as a poet.

The poem has very little in the way of concrete action. Stanzas 1-6 consist of a description of the map, which is an "A-Z street-map" and is in indelible ink, like a "birthmark, tattoo".

The description relates a series of familiar landmarks, and what "she knew"- images of the gravestones in the churchyard, sitting on a bench as a wedding service ends, following someone you know in the rain, waving at departing trains, observing conkers falling on to the pavements, and memories of watching particular films- which appeal to younger teenagers- in the cinema.

The subject matter here is related from a child's point of view ("your tiny face"); those who have died are "like old print/ on a page", while you wonder- in very simple language- about your own future marriage and death; "tasting future time/ on the tip of your tongue". This tone continues in stanzas 7 and 8, with throwing a tennis ball against a wall, and the sounds of ice cream vans, the motorway and "children's shrieks".

The start of stanza 7 says that the protagonist no longer lives there- she seems to be constantly on the move, and constantly elsewhere (why this is so is not explained). There is a reminder that the map is "under" her clothing, a link to stanza 1 which catalogued what clothing she covers the map "with" "when she went out". This recurs at the start of stanza 10, when she gets dressed and goes out.

The emphatic, multi-lingual goodbyes in the last line of stanza 8 mark an end to the childhood in the poem. In stanza 10, she starts to move on from the "one-way street of her past"; travels abroad and speaks a foreign language; acquires a lover; these actions show she has become grown up.

In stanza 11, she "hired a room with a view"- this is an allusion to EM Forster's 1908 novel about a young English girl who goes to Italy and grows up as a result. After such an experience, returning to your childhood home becomes a "façade" because you have changed and your home town has changed. In architecture, a façade can be a false front added to a building (to make it look grander or older, perhaps) - this is a skin deep disguise of what lies behind it.

Snakes and lizards shed their skin when they have outgrown it. Lizards do so in pieces, but a skin shed by a snake is in one piece, turned inside out. Alliteration involving "s" abounds in stanzas 12 and 13- stripped/slept/skin/sloughed/ snake's.

The childhood clothing of leggings and trousers or jeans in stanza 1 become the adult stockings and gloves in stanza 7; in stanza 12, she takes those items off, sleeps, and her skin is shed. In stanza 13, the new skin which has emerged from under the old one is unmarked, and she will have to grow into it; this new, unmapped territory feels to her as though "it belonged to someone else".

The bare narrative therefore involves a young woman with "baby-blue eyes" who goes abroad, from her home town, and has adult experiences, during which the map (because it is losing its grip on her) "seethed"- a little like Armitage's chainsaw- and "perspired".

When she goes back to the town, the map is no longer accurate or relevant- it is no help to her now in "wondering where to go next". While she sleeps, the map is cast off and she finds herself in a new skin i.e. ready for new experiences which are no longer rooted in her childhood identity. The sense at the end of the poem is that she will no longer go back; she is no longer the map woman.

Much of the poem is about modes of transport, and about journeys, which stop being local, and on foot, and become international, by plane; the trains in stanza 5, the map in stanza 10 and the motorway in stanza 8 are personified.

The longer the journeys, the more independent the map woman becomes. This is also a function of time- time to start/ future time/ then/ one day/ next. The poem is narrated in the past tense because the map woman has shed the feeling that her identity comes from growing up where she did.

The poem was published in 2008, just over a century after Forster's novel. It comes from a collection called "Feminine Gospels" i.e. some truths about being a woman.

The map woman is a lone character- she seems to have no family, no particular home, and her occupation is not defined. She is therefore an archetype- she stands for all women, who face the need to find for themselves an identity focused more confidently on where they are going, and what they are growing into, than where they have been and where they came from.

Ian Duhig   The Lammas Hireling

This is a poem in 4 stanzas of 6 lines; the regularity suggests that the experience it contains is ordered, tidy, settled; but in fact it is the opposite of this.

At the end of the poem, we find that the poem is not a soliloquy or a dramatic monologue but a confession addressed to a priest- and that the confession is made hourly (because the narrator feels so guilty, and cannot move on from the images which haunt him).

The story is that the narrator, a farmer, hired a labourer at the Lammas fair (which would be on 1 August, at the end of harvesting). He was (suspiciously) cheap to hire. The cattle prospered under his care, while the farmer liked the fact that he did not talk all the time. The opening stanza is dominated by calculations and economics. The farmer thinks that he has obtained a talented employee at a favourable price; it is almost too good to be true.

The hireling is so inexpensive because he is in fact- or so the farmer thinks- a spirit who can imitate or embody the voice of the late wife. Her voice is "torn"; this implies that she had died in pain (possibly in childbirth?) but the details are left out of the text. An alternative reading of lines 7-8 is that, in his dream or in real life, his dead wife is crying out to the hireling. It may be that the priest to whom the farmer speaks is familiar with the family's history.

55

The farmer dreamt or thought that either the hireling is a devil which embodies the voice of his dead wife; or that his dead wife had been having an affair with him. He believes that the cowherd was a warlock (a male witch and shapeshifter) who will adopt the shape of a hare ("cow with leather horns"), which, in folklore, is devilish. The farmer shot him, out of superstitious belief; the dead farmhand metamorphosed into a hare (stanza 3), and the farmer found that when he carried the dead body in a sack it grew lighter and dropped into the river without a sound. This was clearly supernatural; since then, his herd of cattle is accursed.

There is a wonderful sense of suspense and mystery across the ends of line 20 and the start of line 21. We read "There was no" and we have to look down and left for the "Splash" which never comes, although, as we read the line, we ae waiting for it!

The farmer's language is full of colloquialisms, dialect and references to folklore which he does not explain- they are simple, violent and powerful, like the farmer himself. The verbs the farmer uses are often violent- struck/dropped/ shut up/ hunted/ biting/dropped/casting.

The force (and horror) of the action is conveyed through similes (fat as cream/ fur over like a stone mossing/ eyes rose like bread). The farmer 's dream incited him to murder; now he is an insomniac who spends "all my days" at the confessional. He feels marked by the devil, cursed like his animals. Money is a theme in the first and last stanzas; the farmer who thinks he has got a good bargain finds out that he has lost more than money. He has lost his wife and he has almost lost his mind.

Alliteration features (doted/dropped/doubled; disturbed/dreams/dear/down/dark; lovely/lip/like/lighter). "There was no/Splash" uses the pause at the end of the line to delay the (missing) sound.

The farmer is a simple man, and his diction matches his character. There is only one word of three syllables in the poem- the final word, "confession". Out of 208 words in the poem, an astonishing 175, or 84%, are simple monosyllables, and the rest have two syllables.

Ian Duhig wrote the collection from which this poem comes when he was pursuing an interest in the folktales of the north east of England; the poem could well be a rendition of a folk tale. It is, in that sense, like Agbabi's "Eat Me". Comparisons with the Ford, Duffy and Minhinnick poems would be interesting; mermaids, snakes and foxes could almost conceivably feature in the dreams of Duhig's farmer, too. A more direct link is with Vicki Feaver's "The Gun", which explores the unexpected consequences of hunting and killing, and the primeval aspects of the rural world, with its potential for the unexplained and the supernatural.

Helen Dunmore   To My Nine-Year-Old Self

This poem is in six stanzas of irregular lengths (5,6,7, 6,5 and 3 lines). The narrator speaks to her younger self, using the pronouns you...we.....I.

Stanzas 1-3 each have two sentences, and end at the end of a sentence. Stanzas 4 and 5 run on into stanza 6. There isn't a rhyme scheme; the poem is presented as a (surreal) conversation between the adult narrator and herself as a child. Rhyme would be an artificial method of organising this, and a distraction.

The theme is that we are connected to our childhood by memories, and by the fact that we still have the same body that we had as a child. The idea that we can really meet and have a conversation with our younger self is a surprise.

Each stanza contains an image (or memory) from the summer in which the narrator was aged nine. Most of them are about being in a state of constant movement (balancing, run, walk, climb, leap, jump, hide, lunge).

Stanza 3 implies that there was a dream, as a 9-year-old, and an intention to write it down ; but at this age children are easily distracted, as they have a short attention span. "That summer of ambition" produced a wasp-trap, a way of making ice cream and a den- not exactly a coherent plan or a dream achieved. When the child does concentrate- right at the end of the poem- it is on something you can feel and taste- the

58

scab on a grazed knee (compare, with this, the adult "scars" and the stiffness with which the adult moves in stanza 2).

The adult voice speaks to the child in the language of an adult relationship break-up (forgive me/ that dream we had/ I'd like to say that we could be friends/I won't keep you/ I leave you) - as though the narrator feels that the way she has grown away from her child-self is essentially the same as other "failed" relationships; there is a touch of humour about this, because it is both inevitable and right that we should grow up from our pre-teen selves.

There is a series of images- childhood activities- some of which are innocent (baby vole, sherbet lemons, picking rosehips), one of which is mildly risky (lunge out over the water/ on a rope) and one is dangerous- hiding from paedophiles. Note that "scared lanes" is a transferred epithet- lanes can't be scared, but the narrator can, and she laments, as an adult, that "God knows/ I have fears enough for us both". The awareness of danger, and anxiety about childhood, is a preoccupation of adults. Adults are cautious (stanza 2). Children have no concept of danger- the "ripe scab" is an object of curiosity, not a deterrent to jumping out of windows or swinging on ropes over water.

Our childhood, and the intensity of it, cannot be brought back- the disappearance of the tree "long buried in housing" symbolises this.

The adult is apologetic, and feels at a disadvantage. It is a humorous conceit that the nine-year-old version of ourselves still has an independent and real life, frozen in time. The imagery manages to evoke the flitting of a child from one physical outdoor experience to another; the poem suggests that the emotional intensity of young children is enviable, particularly once we are adults with a plethora of fears, scars and a bad back. **There is a link here with the attitude to the intensity of our experience in Tim Turnbull's "Ode on a Grayson Perry Urn".**

Adults' anxieties are also a theme in Burnside's poem.

UA Fanthorpe   A Minor Role

Ursula Fanthorpe (1929-2009) was a teacher of English for 16 years, before becoming a medical receptionist. She therefore uses her own linguistic resources to give a voice to people who are less articulate. She is often critical, in a humorous way, of how we allow ourselves to be dominated by others who have power over us- not just the medical profession, as here, but, for example, job interviewers (search out her poem "You will be hearing from us shortly").

This dramatic monologue explores the issue of polite self-effacement, and how we tend to avoid confronting the truth, and our embarrassing and uncomfortable feelings, about life, death and chronic illness. Adam Thorpe's "On her Blindness" has a similar theme.

The speaker likes to be unobtrusive and inoffensive. She stands on stage, with minimal lines to deliver, but, five lines from the end of the poem, she throws the spear away, no longer prepared to settle for "a minor role". No longer accepting "my servant's patter", she throws away "the servant's tray", because she is no longer so shy and voiceless as to say almost nothing. In the face of a health crisis- it is ambiguous whose- she is ready, finally, to cast off this cloak of deference, and take centre stage, at least for the time it takes to deliver the clear and impassioned message which closes the poem.

The metaphor of the theatrical performance opens and concludes the poem. The speaker seems to be acting a very small part in a production of Sophocles' "Oedipus Rex".

There is no firm indication that she has anyone else in her life- only "the cat". If we read the poem from this premise, her dialogue is with herself, and her mantra is to be inoffensive at all times; she is small and harmless, and inconsequential.

She refuses to feel sorry for herself, although she knows that all's not well (a reference, perhaps, to Shakespeare's comedy "All's well that ends well"- a cancer diagnosis is unlikely to end well). She wards off "well-meant intrusiveness", and holds her hands under magazines, to avoid making any gestures of distress which might betray her discomfort ,or attract attention or sympathy.

Lines 4-6 heighten the narrator's self-built vulnerability. She is so self-conscious that she thinks people will laugh at her if she delivers the few lines in her tiny (or "midget") part incorrectly- we would hope that audiences are more generous than that. She feels oppressed by the "monstrous fabric" of the performance space, as if it is hostile and populated with danger. She walks fast in the street to avoid the risk of being stopped and spoken to. Any real social interaction is painful; she interprets the concern of other people as "well-meant intrusiveness". She answers the phone with care and restraint, and regards both the caller and the phone as impersonal ("what I say to it"); her responses are polite, but guarded and self-effacing.

The end of the second stanza extends the concept of subservience; the narrator does not *conduct* the "background music of civility", but merely sustains or supports it.

It is only in the privacy of home that this façade of control, and playing down the seriousness of things, can be set aside. If we "Cancel things, tidy things", we are not doing just housework; we are preparing for (our own) death by "putting our affairs in order". There is a sense of pathos here, precisely because the uncomplaining narrator does not feel sorry for herself. Finding comfort in a familiar domestic routine, however dull it is, may be the only way of coping with a bad diagnosis; we sleep and read and cat-stroke our way towards our own inevitable death because there is nothing else to do. This narrator has an aversion to bucket lists, because they would be a form of self-indulgence, showing off.

The poem is clever in weaving together three different themes and settings; the theatrical strand, the picture of a modest domestic existence, and the endless visits to hospital, which are the real material of the "monstrous fabric", in lines 8-13 and 31-33.

It is a relief when this passive, malleable, longsuffering narrator finally finds a spark of defiance. The two uses of the pronoun "you", in line 15 and the last line of the poem, simultaneously do two things. The first is a powerful direct address to the reader , which tells us not to be so accepting of illness and being patronised by the professionals who treat it, and urges us to overcome our innate reluctance to open up to people with our feelings and fears (out of our anxiety that they will laugh at us). The second effect of the use of "you" is that it also reads as part of the narrator's self-talk, in that the poem is as much a confessional directed inwards to herself as it is to the reader. The last line works as an admonition to herself.

There is, though, a further layer of complexity in this poem. It is possible that the narrator is holding hands (under the old, out of date hospital waiting room magazines) with another person; that the hunger-striker and novel- reader is another person; that the cancer diagnosis applies not to the narrator, but to another, unidentified, almost invisible, voiceless person whom the narrator is looking after.

The minor role extends to the carer/sufferer relationship, and the acting analogy fits the domestic situation snugly. This way of reading the poem adds bite to lines 34-35. No-one would choose to play the "star part" when that involves a fatal illness. The exhortation in the last line of the poem is addressed to the ill relative or partner; it is both powerful and powerless at the same time. It affirms that living- even if the quality of that life is compromised- is better than dying; but the sufferer may not be persuaded of that so easily.

Fanthorpe's use of structure is always clever and effective. The poem gradually loses its grip, with lines 18-19 and 33-34 breaking apart- in the second instance, without orthodox punctuation, but even with a capital letter in the middle of the sentence.

"Making sense/ Of consultants' monologues" pauses, at the end of line 10, because it mimics the processing process; absorbing a specialist's monologue takes a few moments of reflection. Similarly, "Being referred/ Somewhere else" (lines 31-

32) gives us the short hiatus we experience while a referral form is filled in, before an appointment card is given to us.

Finally, the stoical and defiant but fatalistic mood here may have a specifically theatrical context- not Sophocles, but Shakespeare. Who else, apart from the narrator here, adopts a grim and resolute cheerfulness in an ultimately hopeless situation (we know it is hopeless, because the cancelling and tidying acknowledge that death is coming)?

Macbeth. In his final soliloquy, in Act 5 scene 5 of Shakespeare's tragedy, he says that we are all merely actors on the stage of life, for our brief lifetime, our hour in the spotlight of our own production.

Fanthorpe's narrator reveals, through her own dramatic monologue, that she is no Macbeth; but, in affirming life over death, she is, finally, heroic for a while, in her own way. She would never describe her own situation as tragic, because that would be theatrical and vulgar. But we feel that her role is not so midget after all.

Vicki Feaver   The Gun

Born in 1943, Vicki Feaver is interested in bringing out repressed aspects of the female mind, and one technique she uses is to set violence in a domestic context- as she does here.

We are unsure until the start of the final stanza whether it is the narrator who is using the gun, or someone else. The colloquialisms (clean through the head, spring in your step) imply that when the narrator says "you", they mean "I". But the pronoun "I" appears at the start of the final stanza. The possibilities are-

1   the narrator is female and she has a male partner who has brought a gun and shoots animals with it
2   the narrator is female, has brought the gun, shoots animals with it and helps someone else with the cooking
3   the narrator is male, uses the gun to shoot animals, and joins in the cooking
4   the narrator is male, a female partner uses the gun, and he joins in the cooking
5   both the shooter and the cook are of the same gender

In bringing a house alive, the gun is presented as restoring excitement to a relationship which has gone stale- it is, at least for the shooter, exciting to be able to take the lives of animals and birds, "like when sex was fresh". It brings out the animal!

The extended simile and image which takes up the final five lines of the poem is very striking. All of this slaughter brings out of the backwoods the King of Death, "his black mouth sprouting golden crocuses".

In Greek literature (and in Tennyson's "Oenone" of 1833) the yellow or golden crocus is used as the carpet of the Gods- Gods like Bacchus- and it is said, in Homer, to be able to set the earth on fire. Bringing the King of Death out of the winter woods to feast on the kill is a disturbing prospect.

The language of the poem combines the quietly domestic and the energetically violent. We have a house, a table, a fridge, a garden, a kitchen, trees, string, tins; and we have a gun, which is described objectively and in a matter of fact way- metal, barrel, gun, stock, grainy, polished, shot.

The dynamism comes in all the words which end in – ing; stalking, bringing, jutting, casting, perforating, dangling, cooking, jointing, slicing, stirring, tasting. The majority of these are culinary terms which only take on a sinister and unpleasant flavour in the context of the dispassionate shooting (clean through the head) of the rabbit.

If the shooting promotes a sense of euphoria "like when sex was fresh", it, too, is energetic and messy- it involves fur, feathers and entrails. But most of us see the aim of sex as affirming life, warmth and romance- not death. The narrator here is like

Carson's in "Balaklava"- carried away with the power and the potential of armed violence.

The paradox is that the gun, the instrument of death, which brings the King of Death out of the woods, itself looks "like something dead"; and that it brings a house alive.

The alliteration of words starting with "f"- first/from/ fridge/ fills/ flown/fur/feathers/fresh/ feast- is notable, and they are almost all monosyllables.

Why is the gun described, in line 6, as "jutting over the edge" of the kitchen table? Because it will take the repressed enjoyment of killing game "over the edge"; it may begin innocently enough, but it becomes so frenzied and addictive that it seems to need a frantic, constant effort to make space in the kitchen for more kills. There are so many that the King of Death comes to feast on them. Killing game, in a sense, becomes a killing game- a game of killing, not for food, but for thrills, while the creatures killed cannot escape or fight back. While this poem presents that as a given, a fact of life, other poets- Ford and Szirtes- prompt us to stand up for the creatures that have been shot.

We can also interpret the gun as a symbol for other forms of excitement, including domestic (and possibly sexual) violence. We are used to "death" having a second meaning in literature, as a euphemism for orgasm (there is an attribution of this meaning to the French phrase *petit mort* in 1882, and it is common in Elizabethan literature- for instance in John Donne's poem "The Legacie").

The "King of Death" may therefore be shorthand for sex of a particularly satisfying kind; this links with the association of the gun, fresh sex and fresh kills in stanza 4. The excitement in the final stanza, and the culinary activities, may carry a sexual undertone.

Vicki Feaver's interest in finding common ground between the genders extends here to the possibility that some women are as gratified by violence as some men. Perhaps she would suggest that one or more of the group which kills the mermaid in Ford's "Giuseppe" should have been a woman.

Leontia Flynn – The Furthest Distances I've Travelled

This poem is a dramatic monologue in eight stanzas of four or five lines. It comprises four sentences, of which the last is only one line long. The first sentence takes up the first three stanzas; the second, two and a half stanzas; the third, almost the same length again.

The poem is in rhyming couplets throughout. Some of the rhymes are forced; the word anonymity is broken in half, in stanza three. This stress in maintaining a rhyme scheme is like maintaining a forced smile for the sake of keeping up appearances.

The tone is optimistic at first, but the high spirits evaporate, as the dream of wandering the world (albeit only in Eastern Europe) collapses. Half way through the poem, at the start of stanza five, we find that the narrator is in the UK, at a post office, alternately unemployed (a giro) or in chronic debt (a handful of bills); having to take her "overdue laundry" to a launderette, and being evicted from one temporary home after another. The list of domestic "souvenirs" is a collection of "crushed valentines"- moments of affection from the past, which do not sustain the practical needs of day to day life.

The conclusion is an extension of the poem's title- "the furthest distances I've travelled have been those between people". Who are these people, and what are these distances?

The discovery of "alien pants" each time she moves suggests that the narrator has short-lived, casual relationships which yield nothing much to remember them by. Possibly, she finds the times (or "distances") between these relationships as far apart- psychologically as much as in literal geography- as travelling thousands of miles.

She has found that the trek of the solo traveller offers freedom of a sort; but she gave it up, because of the "scare stories" that the anti-malarial drug "Larium" (Leontia Flynn uses the alternative spelling) was banned/investigated for its side effect of psychosis and the risk of suicide which taking it might expose her to.

The final stanza indicates that the narrator remains a work-shy free spirit, uninterested in living an orderly or settled life. But life is not so jokey now.

In line 1, she "saddled a rucksack"; in fact, we saddle a horse, but we carry a rucksack. In lines 2-4 she depicts herself as carrying a heavy burden- as if she is a horse. In line 6, the phrase "off the beaten track" becomes "on the beaten track".

The verbal playfulness continues in stanza 2. The Siberian white is a mutant tiger (whose existence has not been proved scientifically), and white cells are the blood cells which protect us against infection. There is no attempt at all to find a rhyme for "white"- the only time in the poem this occurs.

Stanza 3 tells us that the narrator learnt from travelling that her destiny lay "in restlessness"; hence her continuing shiftlessness and inability to live a more settled life. The talk of packing hastily (as if to catch a bus, but really to go and do some washing) and of souvenirs, which are just trivial relics of past nights and conversations, is a half-hearted effort to maintain the myth of a life of freedom, against the most prosaic reality of serial evictions and unemployment.

She sees her relationships in the drab surroundings she inhabits now as short holidays in other people's lives. Her workless life is a continuous holiday, of sorts, although it makes Lithuania, or a Greyhound bus, seem glamorous. Most of us would say that neither of them is.

The poem is rather like Sue Boyle's; it shows us how a young woman can be unprepared for the reality of adult life, and be caught in romantic dreams which are not realistic.

It also belongs among the group of poems which deal with the process of growing up- by Copus, Doshi, Duffy, Dunmore- all of them, coincidentally, female poets.

Roderick Ford   Giuseppe

Although the genesis of this poem lies ostensibly in a story the narrator was apparently told by his/her

Uncle Giuseppe, it is dominated by the strange, symbolic mermaid, and the cruelty done to her.

Sicily is the home of the Mafia, a culture of gang violence; and World War Two features in the poem as the agent of starvation, and of a casual savagery which is extended to the mermaid as it would be to anyone else in armed combat (though she is not a combatant).

We find out, very late in the poem, that the uncle is the keeper of the aquarium in which the mermaid is kept captive. Uncle Giuseppe has told his nephew/niece (the narrator of the poem) that in the face of starvation actions which would otherwise be regarded as wrong can be excused or forgiven. A deputation including a fishmonger, a doctor and a priest came to kill the mermaid. They lied, in saying that she/it had been found on the beach. The mermaid is not washed up on the shore, and she is not the kind of fish a fisherman might catch or find; she is a helpless captive, in a man-made aquarium.

The priest said that "she was only a fish", but stanza three raises the issue of whether the incubation of a roe makes this infanticide; or can you commit infanticide against an unborn fish? Are unhatched fish eggs a viable form of life?

A mermaid is a mythical creature with the tail of a fish but the head, arms and trunk of a woman. It is, then, in a sense both a fish and a woman, but the priest denies her status or identity as a woman. There are clues which guide us to treat her firstly as a woman- she has a wedding ring. Fish do not have their throats cut, or their heads and hands buried; they are cut up on a fishmonger's slab, not on the ground in a courtyard; and they neither scream nor convey a sense of fear, because they are inexpressive.

The presence of a priest here is interesting. This is a Catholic priest (because Sicily is a Catholic country), who, we might expect, will (presumably) administer the last rites to the dying mermaid; but, instead, he condones the murder, or butchery. The excuse that she is "only a fish" did not really persuade Uncle Giuseppe, who cannot "look me in the eye" as he retells the tale- out of guilt or shame or embarrassment.

In 1943, British, American and Canadian troops launched a major invasion of Italy via Sicily. Casualty figures are hard to quantify because very large numbers of troops were missing but it seems to have been in the order of 100000. Two American soldiers were found guilty of war crimes when they shot captured Italian and German troops at Biscari.

The name Giuseppe translates as Joseph, and we are familiar with the concept of the archetypal American soldier being referred to as "GI Joe". One of the foremost Mafiosi in Sicily was Giuseppe Genco

Russo (1893-1976). The name Giuseppe is non-specific, but plenty of Giuseppes have been involved in unlawful violence down the decades.

The fact that we have no detail by which to define the mermaid, the priest or the other characters, and no means of identifying the location of the aquarium, suggests that we are dealing here with archetypes. More specifically, the poem raises questions about the oppression of women, and the scope for masculine cruelty towards (pregnant/ married?) women, in a Catholic country, and, by extension, in any country.

If the mermaid is more woman than fish, then the violence perpetrated here is not just murder but cannibalism too. If all that is left is a head and her hands, then her body- which is part human- has been "cooked and fed to the troops". The type of murder which is presented here so graphically as a form of butchering, accompanied by screaming, is something we may associate with a Mafia-type execution, but Mafia killings have always been mainly of men by men.

The story Uncle Giuseppe tells feels like a fable, or a fairy tale gone wrong. In some cultures, mermaids are a harbinger of bad luck.

Sicily certainly suffered once it became a World War 2 battlefield, and one result of the Allied occupation was the resurgence of the Mafia, which Mussolini had tried to suppress. The Mafiosi include men whose occupations are "fishmonger, and certain others", and the poem may be saying, on one level, that, in the history of Sicily, the Catholic Church has been passively endorsing its violence.

Shelley's poem "Ozymandias" similarly puts someone else, **not the narrator**, at its heart; Shelley uses "a traveller" to convey to the narrator of the poem an account and an interpretation of a scene which may or may not be relied upon by this narrator, and therefore by the reader. Giuseppe is the keeper of the aquarium, so he had handed the mermaid over to those who wanted to kill her; the poem is a confessional on his part.

While the imagery in stanza 2 is graphic, the tone of the poem is cold and matter-of-fact; there is little emotional involvement in the telling of the poem, because the act of telling it is modulated by guilt. **There are parallels here with Duhig's "The Lammas Hireling"**; a murderer may be able to justify his act to himself, but he will have to live with the guilt of it afterwards.

The mermaid- "she, it"- is depersonalised by those who want to kill and eat her. **There is an obvious connection here with Patience Agbabi's poem "Eat me", which achieves a similar allegorical effect.**

The mermaid must have a core significance to the poem, and so must the setting, in Sicily. The lack of specific geographical detail which would allow us to identify the location (such as the town of Stafford, in Carol Ann Duffy's "The Map-Woman") challenges us to find a broader meaning. Sicily has been a battleground and the home of the Mafia, with its exploitation and "protection" of people, and its overt reverence for women. The Church is a respected and prominent- even authoritative- institution in the life of its people, and is an accessory to murder here.

The mermaid is not *only* or *just* a fish. She or it is recognisably human, through its physical features (hands and feet) and its terrified screams and its wedding ring. The "starvation" the men are experiencing leads them to kill and eat her, persuading themselves that she is just a fish. This implies that the poem presents us with a view that **it is easy for women to be treated as less than human, when men are starved.**

The mermaid's killers are all men, as far as we can tell. The mermaid has been kept in captivity, and it is only the starvation which motivates the murder itself and the excuses for it. Leaving the wedding ring on her severed hand, and Giuseppe's sense of shame in the final stanza, indicate that the excuses do not convince those who make them. In a culture of violence, women will be particular victims of domestic violence, and they are powerless to avoid it.

Roderick Ford has kindly corresponded with me on this poem.
He says that he wrote the poem after he had read a comment that the people of Sicily were so short of food during the War that they ate all the fish in the aquarium, including the mermaid.

The mermaid is and is not human; she has no advocate, and shares this vulnerability with many other minorities, of many different kinds. The poem explores the difficult question of whether the community should protect the voiceless, or whether, in extreme circumstances, it is justified to sacrifice the weak.

Whereas Szirtes' "Song" asserts that the oppressed have and will always find a voice, this poem is less optimistic that the balance of power will tend to be corrected.

Roderick Ford tells me that there is an allegorical link between the mermaid and Christ; both are **forced to accept their own sacrifice** in order to save others.

Regarding the form of the poem, the irregular lengths of the stanzas are designed, he says, to reflect the uncertainty of things in wartime, and to point up each part of the action, so that we have to face it squarely, and not evade it.

In this way, both the nephew (or niece) and the uncle are making judgments about a shocking past event- one where there are mitigating circumstances, but still an inhumane deed. The question for the reader is therefore whether, faced with the same crisis of starvation, we would do the same.

This poem is unusual within the collection of 28, because it presents a personal dilemma. **Doshi's** poem presents the difficulty of humanitarian aid, emigration and adoption, but from the point of view of the consequences of it, not the initial choice. **Burnside's** poem explores the instinct for a nation to seek revenge for a terrorist outrage, to assert its values, where it could choose a path of tolerance and plurality. That dilemma is a nationalistic one, just as **Szirtes'** poem is about the political arena. *It is only Ford and Duhig who put the personal conscience under the poetic microscope.*

Seamus Heaney   Out of the Bag

Heaney (1939-2013) was one of the best known and most popular poets of his generation. This long poem (ninety-four lines, in stanzas of three lines throughout, except for the stand-alone line 37) deals with what Heaney calls "incubation", in the dual senses of childbirth and the genesis of poetry (for a more direct poet's view of the process of the birth of a poem, you may like to read Ted Hughes' "The Thought Fox").

The narrator relates his own experience of being born, subjectively and retrospectively, in the final, fourth section, from lines 80-94, and surreally, in lines 14-37.

The first 13 lines are concerned with the doctor's bag- and, by implication, the title of the poem. We talk about "letting the cat out of the bag", meaning allowing secrets to come out into the open.

The secret here is what Heaney asserts as the magical power of poetry, which has healing properties, because there is something mysterious in its genesis and creation- it is as miraculous as human birth.

The first part of the second section (lines 38-67) is autobiographical; it relates an episode when the 16-year-old Heaney experienced a hallucination at a religious procession; a hallucination regarding his own birth.

Doctor Kerlin therefore occupies lines 1-37 and lines 56-65, and the final stanza. The other kind of doctor is the "poeta doctus", the poet and classical scholar, who has researched the mystical medicinal powers which the ancient Greeks attributed to poetry.

Heaney relates his hallucination at Lourdes- a place of pilgrimage, which is thought by Roman Catholics to be a place of healing- to Epidaurus, which was thought to be the birthplace of Asclepius, the son of Apollo, and was a centre of healing in ancient Greece. People would sleep there for a night and the God of healing (Asclepius) would   supposedly reveal to them in their dreams what they should do to recover their health.

The theatre at Epidaurus has famously fine acoustics, and the medium Greek playwrights used was verse, not prose. Heaney suggests that the theatre was part of the "cure" at Epidaurus; that poetry has the power to cure illness. Taken at face value, this idea is as hallucinatorily outlandish as the cartoon-like aspects of Doctor Kerlin, but the argument is that poetry may be as divine as the God of healing.

The fourth stanza of section 2 points out that the word "incubation" has more than one meaning. We put premature babies in incubators ("incubating for real", line 86), but the archaic meaning derives from the Latin "incubus". That is a form of spirit possession while you are asleep (the cowherd in Duhig's poem is a very good example of this).

In modern English, we associate this with evil spirits, but lines 46-48 show us that this is a healing, not an illicit "epiphany". The childbirth at the end of the poem is conducted in sleep (or under anaesthesia). Birth is a triumph and an occasion for smiles.

Hygeia is the daughter of Asclepius and the goddess of cleanliness. The Doctor spends much of his time washing his hands (lines 2-4, 19-23, 62-63) and playing with condensation (lines 56-61), and Epidaurus has sanitary baths (line 46), just as the waters at Lourdes are thought by some to have healing properties.

The Doctor switches the light off and "darkens" the door when he leaves (line 12), and the goddess Hygeia "undarkens" the world of illness. The poem proposes that Hygeia and Doctor Kerlin are far apart in time, but connected in purpose; and when the narrator revisits the room in which he was born (in section 4), the vivid images connect his adult self with his infant self.

The Doctor is an ever-present in the narrator's family, on hand whenever any of "all of us" is born; he delivers well-being, like Asclepius. Although Kerlin is a genuine surname, it is also an anagram of "linker"; the narrator's experience at Lourdes and/or Epidaurus in sections 2 and 3 links poetry and healing.

The notion that dreams and memories can be as real as reality (incubation in the ritual sense versus incubating for real), and the elision of the Doctor from obstetrician to cartoonist in steam, as well as the comparison of him with a hypnotist (line 8), makes it easier for the reader to accept the central premise of the poem- "the cure/ By poetry".

The Doctor is depicted as a godlike figure from an alien world (Hyperborean means the far North), a world of ice (line 30) and cold (line 33), and of clinical whiteness; he stitches babies together, assembling them from "infant parts"- rather like "the city of spare hearts", with its storerooms full of hearts, in Sylvia Plath's poem "The Stones".

Line 82 suggests that the poem is about what survives "the passage of time"; "the room I came from and the rest of us all came from" is "pure reality", but there is another kind of reality, here, in dreams and hallucinations. The desire to die (in stanzas 3 and 4 of section 3) is juxtaposed with the birth/bedroom in section 4; the sheets unite birth, marriage and death- the whole of a human life.

The poem compresses time and belief, from the ancient world to ours. It uses the Doctor as a symbol of continuity, and it argues that modern poetry has the same healing power as Epidaurus, which relied not just on its sanatorium, but on its theatre, to give its visitors their "epiphany"- their encounter with the gods. The other poem which explores the mysteries of creativity, and the need for it, is Minhinnick's poem.

Alan Jenkins   Effects

The title of this poem has a double meaning, which only becomes clear in the last of its 50 lines. It means the personal effects of the speaker's mother, which are returned to him by nurses after his mother has died. The poem is also about the "effects" on him of her death and his memories of her.

The poem is continuous, and it consists of just two sentences, the first of which ends in line 15, while the second runs to the end of the poem.

The poem is a dramatic monologue, a stream of consciousness, voiced at the key moment where the narrator comes back to see his mother, only to find that she has died. It also serves as a memorial or biography of her, especially her more recent times, in which she had become increasingly vulnerable, dependent and sad.

The hand-holding in line 1 acquires new resonance and meaning when we reach line 44, and then again at the close of the poem, which ends at the same time as her life has ended. The subtle shift in the phrasing- "I held her hand" to "the hand I held"- mirrors the narrator's feelings of guilt, and his sense, now, that he has been too self-centred and has neglected her. He has, belatedly, developed a new perspective, which is more understanding of her needs- but it is too late now. It is only by her dying that he has addressed his inadequacies as a son.

Lines 1-8 present the scene in the kitchen when he was a child; line 6 hints that this family was always undemonstrative, emotionally reserved. It presents the mother as hard-working, poor and conservative in her tastes and attitudes, always preferring the familiar to the alternative (like the miners in O'Brien's "Fantasia"). This opening vignette is an independent section of the poem, with a rhyme scheme ABCABDDB; it is a childhood memory, but it needs to be attached to the rest of the poem, because the narrator's stream of thought is continuous.

Lines 9-16 take us forward (how far in time, we are not told) to her life as a widow. Again, there is a focus on the mother's hands, because, after being widowed, she had put her rings away, along with other commonplace items of sentimental value. This implies that, sadly, she found it painful to wear them, either from grief or perhaps from disappointment; she did not wish to be identified as the wife of the man she had married. The precise reason for that way of thinking has ceased to matter, we will come to feel, once we realise that she, too, is, now, dead.

The theme of financial insecurity returns with the disclosure that the family only went abroad on holiday once. The theme of emotional insecurity emerges in lines 14-16; latterly, she had put her rings on again, as if they were a comfort, or would give her respectability, or respect, or would help her to combat acute confusion and loneliness. Wearing them again is an attempt to cling to her sense of who she is. It may be that dementia is destroying that.

The disappearance of her watch in lines 16-18 contrasts with the "thick rubber band" which has replaced it in lines 42-43. The watch is of value, and it denotes that she is an individual, and of value; this differentiation of her from other people disappears in hospital, just like the watch, which she believed the nurses had stolen (lines 34-35).

Lines 9-16 have the rhyme scheme ABACDEEF. As the reality of grief intrudes on his consciousness, the narrator cannot keep as strong a grip, or sense of order, on what he says to us.

From the end of line 16 to line 25, we find a role reversal. Now he, the son, is cooking for his mother, but it is still the bland food she had always cooked (chops and chicken portions are cheap cuts of meat). The alliteration and contrast of "familiar flavours" and "funny foreign" simply highlights the tastes of a particular generation, probably born in the 1920s. These lines rhyme ABBCBCDEF.

Next, we have a seven-line episode in which the mother has become a heavy drinker out of chronic loneliness. She "stared unseeing….stared" because she realised that, in the absence of visits from her son/children, there was just emptiness in her life. She tried to revive the connection with her late husband, which she had previously set aside, by drinking the whisky he had drunk and which she had never drunk. The verbs here convey the sheer emptiness of her daily life, and the severity of the struggle just to keep moving- heaved/blinked/poured/gulped/stared.

After the rhyming couplet at lines 26-27, the rhyme scheme collapses, as she loses all direction and sense of purpose in her life. Interestingly, regularity, in the form of rhyme, returns as soon as she goes into the rigid, regimented hospital in line 33. The rhymes from there to the end of the poem are tight and biting- in lines 34-41, the pattern is ABCBDADC, and the rhymes are dreamt/contempt; before/swore; blared/stared; and, daringly (because of their alleged dishonesty and lack of care) nurses/curses.

Lines 42-50 are even more claustrophobic- ABABCCDDD; band/hand; wore/more (carrying over from before/swore); sleeve/leave; and finally she/see/me- because she could not see the narrator to say goodbye, when she most wanted to.

Some of the rhymes bind the poem together across the various episodes- scarred/hard/ ward in lines

1/4/33; bland (22)/ hand (44); disdain (20)/ again (32); watch (16)/ scotch (30); abroad (13)/ poured (29); and so on.

The progressive episodes of decline in his mother's life are also part of the entity of a single, continuous lifetime, in which structure and purpose existed when she was a mother, weakened when she was a widow, and was imposed when she became a psychiatric patient. Her growing incomprehension is realised through the action of her eyes- stared unseeing/blinked/stared/blinked unseeing/ blinked and stared/ she could not........see. From line 26 onwards- for exactly half of the poem- she is unable to process visual clues, and a rapid physical and mental decline follows her isolation. Her hand can grip at the start of the poem, but not from line 42 onwards.

It is authentic, in terms of psychology, to say that at some point quite late in our lives we start to relate our experience to our past rather than to our future. Memories of the past occupy the space we used to reserve for our hopes and plans for the future. This poem is a remarkably crafted and poignant illustration of that truth.

The narrator has returned to the hospital too late; just as with "all the weeks I didn't come", he alludes to his sense of guilt and unreliability, without labouring it. Rather like Ford's mermaid, his mother has been abandoned- but the responsibility, for Jenkins, is the narrator's alone.

"Of course I left" (line 48) is a comment on the way in which children and parents have to disentangle their lives, as they grow older.

The mother's hand, scarred from hard work, poverty and tough love at the start of the poem, becomes, in death, "blotched and crinkled". So, by implication, is her son's conscience and his face; he feels guilty of neglect, and he will be crying with grief.

Robert Minhinnick   The Fox in the National Museum of Wales

Like the mermaid in Roderick Ford's "Giuseppe", this fox has the power to haunt our imaginations long after we have read the poem it inhabits. The fox is a symbol of something; the question is, of what?

We associate foxes (and wolves) with sharp teeth and violent death, predating on chickens (and, in the Little Red Riding Hood fairy tale, grandmothers). Some people regard foxes as dangerous vermin; they kill farm animals, and sneak into houses and attack babies. Yet there is a fox-hunting lobby and an anti-fox-hunting lobby. Some people believe that the fox is not a heartless assassin, but, to borrow a film title (originally Roald Dahl's), the fantastic Mr Fox.

The poem uses the fox to unsettle us- as we would be, if we were in a museum and saw one. The refrain "the fox is in the flock" is a warning, and this fox has "blood on the bristles of his mouth". He (not "it") induces shivers in the vases he touches. But the poem concludes that the fox "is something to follow.....is the future". The fox is characterised as an elegant dancer ("shimmies surreptitiously....at a foxtrot") and an elegant dresser, "shiny as a silver fax in his fox coat". The playfulness of the language **minimises the fox's dangerousness**. Not only is the fox the centre of attention- the word *fox* appears 18 times in the poem- but any and all words beginning with f/ph are celebrated- there are a further nineteen of them.

The fox "has seen so much", and he is **observant**, with a wide-ranging, penetrating way of looking at things (lines 3, 12). He is **in perpetual motion** (doesn't stop/ had left/ has swept/ goes/ skedaddles/ moves/ shimmies/ goes/ travels/ further goes), and, specifically, he "never hurries yet passes an age in a footfall". He sees everything, but "No one else has seen him yet"- he is **invisible to everyone except the narrator**. He is **uncivilised**, in the sense of not having undergone a process of civilising, but he is visiting a museum, a place which records the historical process of civilisation, and, in the sweep of an eye and a tail, he takes it all in. The fox's incessant momentum is reinforced by the use of the words backwards/ beneath/ forwards/ behind/ between/ under; the fox somehow **provides continuity and coherence** which link together the hugely varied exhibits and the eras they originate in. Uncivilised himself, he is interested in, and a visitor to, the museum which tells the story of civilisation.

The listing of the contents of the museum is colourful and virtuosic, and the virtuosity extends to the language of the poem; words which sound similar are indulged and exhibited to the reader- porcelain, portrait and pouring; fox, fax, flux, flock; follow, fellow; skeleton, skedaddles; lambs, labyrinth; leatherbacked, legerdemain; fossils, foster; forest, formaldehyde; whale, whalebone.
This consonance in the language is preferred to repetition (of which, apart from the key word "fox", there is very little). Repetition would be heavy-footed, but the playfulness with words is fleet-footed and light, like the protagonist of the poem!

Hearing that the fox is in the museum, the narrator "came as quickly as I could"; he cannot catch up with the fox (lines 46-47), which has been here before (line 22). The narrator is willing to follow the fox, and the fox "is the future".

The poem uses the present tense throughout, to report the movement and progress of the fox. The narrator sets out the fox's whereabouts precisely, and gives them a physical context by specifying which rooms the fox goes out of and into- even though he cannot see the fox because he is always behind him. The fox is apparently both **elusive and purposeful**, but the purpose is left for the reader to speculate on.

The fox is personified, moderately, by being gender-specific, and a museum visitor, but he is not anthropomorphised- he remains very much a fox. He is associated with war, armour and death (lines 30-31) and with death and darkness (lines 21-22), but he is not sinister or aggressive. He comes "from the forest"- not an urban fox, but a visitor from the countryside.

What does the fox symbolise?

I read him as adaptable, a survivor who has seen the whole of history and been present in all of it. He "sniffs at the dodo"- he can scent extinction, but he is not threatened by it. Upheavals leave him untouched, because he is versatile and experienced (he "has seen so much"). He is not delayed or fascinated by the exhibits, by history or art or science; he is not apparently interested in the past (or the future), but only in the present.

This visitor from the forest seems to me to be a visitation to remind us that the planet we live on is much bigger than human history defines it as; that **we**

must adapt to our changing environment, and learn from the simple survival skills and instincts of the fox; and that by looking for what is in nature, found "in the forest", rather than urban or manufactured, we can absorb some of the fox's resilience- a resilience which the playful and energetic language of the poem celebrates, enjoys and admires.

The poem has 60 lines in total, in twelve stanzas which range from four to eight lines each. In the last twenty lines, the focus on the museum weakens and the focus on the fox intensifies; the lines shorten, and the language simplifies. Both real and unreal, the fox seems to be in the museum still; but the iron doors are being shut by those who cannot see him.

Perhaps this indicates that unless we emulate or follow the fox, we will be shut inside our conventional view of the world, through the prism of history, science and the arts; none of which have any intrinsic value in helping us to survive, because the contents of the museum are inanimate objects, and the remains of dead or extinct things.

If we want to avoid our own extinction, we should follow the fox back to the forest, having observed and knowing about the past, but trusting our own ingenuity more, as we seek a strategy to survive in a changing world.

Sinead Morrissey   Genetics

This poem is a villanelle- a poem with a set structure (see Wikipedia for more details of the form and its history). A very famous example is Dylan Thomas' "Do not go gentle into that good night"- another poem written by a child about a parent. This poem seems to consider our position as a child of divorced parents (which Sinead Morrissey is) but it has a surprise for us at the end.

It consists of five stanzas of three lines each, and then one stanza of four lines. Look at the rhyme scheme- it starts ABCCBA, so that the second lines all rhyme-

pleasure/lovers/river/over/register/future.

The last line of each stanza is hands/palms/hands/palms/ hands/hands. The last line of one stanza and first line of the next one rhyme four times out of five-

hands/lands, hands/stands, palms/psalms, hands/demands.

We have four fingers and a thumb, and a palm, on each hand. Is this reflected in the numbers and size of the stanzas (stanzas 1-5 representing a finger, and stanza 6 a palm)?

The repetition of palms and hands may be an allusion to the first meeting of Romeo and Juliet in Shakespeare's play- the iconic image of everlasting romantic love (**the character of Juliet also influences Julia Copus' "An Easy Passage"**).

The poem is about the concept that, even when a marriage ends in divorce, there is a residual, permanent genetic connection; the narrator detects a physical resemblance to each of her parents in the shape of her own hands. This pleases her ("with pleasure"). Stanza 3 contains the language of marriage (togetherness, marriage) and stanzas 4 and 5 locate a wedding scene in a church-chapel/steeple/priest reciting psalms/their wedding. Stanzas 2 and 3, by contrast, contain the language of divorce- repelled, separate, sleep with other lovers, nothing left.
Stanzas 4 and 5 "re-enact their wedding with my hands"- if you put your fingers together in a praying gesture, the shape of your hands as they touch is like a church steeple.

The pronoun "my" features fourteen times; "me" three times; "They/their" five times. Suddenly, and unexpectedly, the pronoun "you" appears in the penultimate line, and "our" and "us" both come into the final line of the poem.

Until now, the poem has seemed to be a soliloquy, but now we find it is addressed to someone to whom the narrator wants to "bequeath", or leave to the next generation, the same kind of genetic handprint, or fingerprint. In this way, the poem becomes about three generations:

* the narrator's parents
* herself
* her children-to-be.

The effect of the language, with its emphasis on our identity being linked so closely to the biology of our family, and the role of the church in recognising marriage down the generations, is to convey the idea that our identity remains intact even when our family does not; relationships are temporary but genetic identity is permanent and cannot be severed. The maternal instinct, too, is stronger than the sense of disappointment when the family you grew up in disintegrates.

The revelation, only at the end of the poem, of the identity of the person to whom it is addressed, **is a technique we find in "The Lammas Hireling" too**.

The idea that "My body is their marriage register" **is a little like the concept of the map woman** - we ourselves are an indelible record of where we have come from, both geographically, for Duffy, and biologically, in this poem.

The inference of the last stanza, taken with the use of the words "wedding" and "marriage" (twice), **is that the poem is really a marriage proposal from the narrator to her partner.** In this way, the genetics, the DNA, will be replicated, again, for and in the next generation.

You could contrast this view of families with the **Copus poem, or Tishani Doshi's "the Deliverer". The poems by Ros Barber and Eavan Boland** also deal with what is passed on from parents to children.

Andrew Motion   From the Journal of a Disappointed Man

The title of this poem derives from the candid diaries with the same title by WNB Barbellion, a pseudonym for BF Cummings (1889-1919), a naturalist with literary and artistic leanings who suffered and died from multiple sclerosis.

There may be a secondary nod in the direction of "The Diary of a Nobody", by George and Weedon Grossmith, serialised in the satirical magazine"Punch", and then published in book form in 1892. It gave us the character of Mr Pooter, a snobbish and self-important hero in his own estimation, but a man, to others, out of his depth and not worth taking much trouble over.

Barbellion's writing is a strange and compelling mixture of self-love, self-absorption and self-loathing. It reads as a desperate, modernistic attempt to make something significant out of a fairly ordinary life. Behind a "timid exterior" he is "embittered, angry, hateful", and although he wants to escape his "life of consummate isolation" and achieve a "fuller life" by making friends, his own personality is an obstacle. Because he has an "idealising yet analytical mind", he admires and likes people, but then finds that they are less pleasant or clever or honest than he thought; "the disappointment dulls the heart".

Andrew Motion's poem is an ironic exploration of self-absorption- the final words "me of course" demonstrate that the narrator is concerned with himself. The narrator complains that the workmen, who have a job to do, are "ignoring me". He is vain. He wants to be the centre of attention, although he is where he deserves to be- on the touchline of this particular game.

Although the poem is a narrative, it has elements of the dramatic monologue; we cannot help developing a strong sense of the narrator's prissy, hyperbolic attitudes. His grandiose use of language (massive, baffled, majesty, Doom, mystic, monsters, abandoned, affair, eclipse, justice) exposes the gap between a very prosaic scene - some workmen manoeuvring a pile on a pier- and his attempt to infuse it with an invented and imaginary significance.

Seeing the workmen is hardly a "discovery"; they are in plain sight. The narrator emphasises the pile, "as I said", and upgrades it from the merely new to "massive". The use of the word "very" in stanza 2 again seeks to exaggerate; either you are silent or you're not; there is no difference, in fact, between being silent and being very silent.

The observations on the lack of speaking in stanza 3 are comical; the monosyllabic instructions are entirely justified, and appropriate to the context. They are not interesting or significant, not worth analysing. The next two stanzas develop the comedy, at the narrator's expense. He cannot identify the nature of the "great difficulty" he believes these massively experienced experts find themselves confronted with, even though he has paid "close attention" to one of them, who is on a ladder, and has detected from that position- standing on the ladder- that there is a "secret problem".

The narrator has wasted "at least an hour" trying to ennoble the project at the pier, and make the workmen pseudo-heroic. The description of the foreman as walking "with a heavy kind of majesty" is reminiscent of Steinbeck's description of the senior farmhand Slim in "Of Mice and Men"- "he moved with a majesty only achieved by royalty and master craftsmen". Smoking a cigarette is a habit, and the explanation that he does so "to relieve the tension" is the narrator's invention- the act itself needs no interpretation. The man is just a cigarette-smoker.

Stanza 7 uses bathos; its aim, to distinguish these (ordinary) men and make them seem heroic by acknowledging, and stressing, that they continued to address the baffling problem, peters out, just as their effort does.

At the end of the poem we have an image of the pile, "still in mid-air"; and the narrator ("and me of course") also suspended in mid-air, both literally, and figuratively, in his futile attempt to over-interpret behaviour. He is no anthropologist. We cannot suspend this narrator in mid-air without laughing at his pretentiousness.

Motion has said that his poems emerge from the tension between a thinking part of a mind which is "conscious, alert, educated and manipulative", and another part, "as murky as a primaeval swamp". The narrator he creates here is a timid bystander, but his admiration for these perfectly ordinary workmen has a latent homo-erotic, or at least an idealising tendency (very powerful men/ monsters/ strong arms). The emphasis on their strength contrasts with the narrator's weakness and timidity, but the workmen give up, too. Their apparent competence is irrelevant because, after a relatively modest effort, they too...................... simply give up.

The narrator tries, consistently, to elevate them in their skills and expertise- all the paraphernalia/ massive style/ all their strength and experience/like a mystic/ original thinker. But the truth is that they cannot think, or cannot be bothered to think, and they walk away from the project, leaving it unfinished. The narrator- like Barbellion- overestimates their qualities, fantasises about their skills, and feels let down when reality intrudes on his fantasy that he is caught up in something important.

The poem is a neat and faithful representation of the experience Cummings/ Barbellion described as his own- "my first impulse is always to credit folk with being nicer, cleverer, more honest and amiable than they are.......I am always finding them out, and the disappointment dulls".

The original Journal of a Disappointed Man is painful to read, but it does not have the ironic dimension Motion brings to this poem; there is no sign that this poem's narrator has a crippling physical disease, but he cannot see the world as it is, and he has a compulsive urge to magnify his own importance and the significance of what he sees in his daily life. He is looking for meaning where none exists.

To some extent, we may all be prone to doing that; and it is even possible that literary analysis and criticism is an exercise which looks too deeply for an explanation of the "secret problem"- a quest it has itself invented, in the sense that it was not in the mind of the creative writer in the first place!

Perhaps the lasting impression is that there are some subjects poetry cannot be made from, and others we should not try to recast in poems. The words at the ends of the lines are prosaic- words like paraphernalia, monosyllables, difficulty, incident. The tension- to borrow a word from stanza ten- is between the banality of the subject matter and the narrator's determination to build it into a poem with him connected to the action.

The poem is in eleven stanzas of four unrhymed lines; eight of them end with a full stop, and one with a semi-colon. The dull predictability of this structure- a structure controlled by the narrator- is subject to only minor variation, in the first four stanzas, where sentences of five lines and three lines do not conform rigidly to the pattern. However, they are still end-stopped sentences. The narrator's rebellion, and his attempts to assert his own, reinventing order over a dull scene, are feeble (like the men's failure to finish the job). He tries to assert himself, but he has nothing to assert.

He cannot turn his dull life into an interesting piece of architecture, because there is nothing striking or creative about it. He is interested in a large block of wood because, in it, he unconsciously recognises a kindred spirit!

There is a natural link between this poem and UA Fanthorpe's "A Minor Role". The difference is that Fanthorpe's narrator is self-aware and unambitious, while Motion's is the opposite. Fanthorpe's poem is about the sad side of feeling self-conscious. Motion's is about the necessity of social embarrassment for a certain personality type who sees himself in the major role when he is, at best, carrying a tray!

Daljit Nagra   Look we have coming to Dover!

The epigraph to this poem, from Matthew Arnold's "Dover Beach", highlights the intense feelings someone landing there may feel. Nagra's poem ends with the word Britannia!, and the poem is about the notions of Britannia (or patriotism, or national identity) which its "natives" have, as well as what it symbolises for immigrants arriving on the coast of Britain- more simply, to begin with, the hope of a better life.

Nagra was born in south-east England but his parents, Punjabi Sikhs, came here in the 1960s as shopkeepers, first in London and then in Sheffield. Nagra says that he is conscious of the fact that the English language has absorbed or assimilated words from a very wide range of countries (because of our sea-faring and empire-running history), and he wanted to catch that multilinguistic tone in this poem- "so various..........".

We are familiar with the figure of Britannia from Thomas Arne's song "Rule Britannia", in which Britannia "rules the waves" and Britons will "never be slaves". Arne's setting of 1740 is still traditionally performed at the Last Night of the Proms, an English cultural tradition. The words were written by the Scottish poet James Thomson and the song/anthem was first performed at an event designed to help the German Prince Frederick to be accepted in English society. Britannia is a figure emblematic of Britain, but created partly for nationalistic reasons and partly as an umbrella for multiculturism. The words "waves" and "free" are in Arne's song, as well as in Nagra's poem; and the elevated language of **prow'd** and **ministered** could almost belong there too.

The five stanzas of five lines narrate the story of the excited arrival and subsequent experiences of immigrants, although they are more likely to arrive at the port of Dover nowadays than to invade the beach (as the Vikings or Normans might have done).

As invaders tend to find, their arrival is cold, wet, hostile and unpleasant. The white chalk cliffs of Dover are the same colour as the "surf", but the surf in stanza one is not sea-water but spittle- in gobfuls, phlegmed; and the rain and wind are released by thunder, which "unbladders" them. In the 1960s and 1970s, when racism was rife in Britain, immigrants were used to being spat on and even urinated on.

Seagulls are aggressive and territorial; "shoal life" is the maritime equivalent of "pond life", which we use as shorthand for the unintelligent. "Vexing" means expressing anger or irritability, and "blarnies" is nonsense or rubbish. The day-trippers who spit in the sea, and the creatures which live in the sea and the sky above it, are all hostile to the incomers. The sense of the idealism being rubbed away from the idealistic dream they have followed extends to the cliffs. They are not flashing clean and white, but "scummed"- a dirty brownish colour- and crumbling.

Having been lashed with high-speed spittle aimed directly at them (brunt), the new arrivals are then verbally abused and beaten up by the "yobbish" weather, rain and wind. Camouflage is used by soldiers in battle, to disguise themselves, but also by animals which seek to escape their predators. As the incomers get beyond the cliffs of Dover, the attacks of the gulls and fish continue. "Scramming on mulch" suggests that they are dispersing over farmland covered in compost or weed-killer. Cold and oppressed, they are "huddled" and "hutched in a Bedford van".

Rabbits are kept in hutches; the Bedford van was a commercial vehicle manufactured by Vauxhall in the 1960s. It was less reliable than the Ford Transit, and was often used as an ice cream van or a mobile shop, by traders who could not afford to trade from rented shop premises. "Rain and wind on our escape" reminds us of the phrase "Raining on your parade"- the idea that hard times or bad luck will dampen people's enthusiasm and spoil their dreams and celebrations.

The third stanza tells the story of the next stage of an immigrant family's integration. They **reap** or **work hard** inland- in towns and cities- unnoticed, and below the radar. The urban myth of the Asian shopkeeper, open all hours, still persists; there is nothing remarkable about these people except their capacity for hard work. But they also receive "stabs in the back"- break-ins, robberies- and they are burdened by ill-health, in an alien climate where rain beats down hard (teemed) and the sun never seems to shine.

Nevertheless, these adversities also ennobled them- and, in the secondary meaning of the word, many Asian entrepreneurs have been made life peers in Britain in recognition of their success. The rhymes of **parks** and **sparks**, and the repetition of **pylon**, suggest a pattern of **power and dynamism which spreads (like the national grid** for transmitting electricity) and sparks into heat and light all over the country.

Stanza four continues to develop the theme of immigrants' unobserved, inconspicuous hard work, out of the spotlight, labouring in the dark, but relying on the eventual payoff of success in the long term.

There are now "Swarms of us"- a phrase which denotes large numbers, but can also be pejorative (swarms of locusts) when used to describe a plague or over-supply. When they become British citizens, because the swarms of immigrants span the rainbow (they are established throughout the spectrum of society), they have a passport... to life, as respectable citizens, and they can emerge into the open, "bare-faced"- no longer huddled, hutched, camouflaged, unseen. We associate "bare-faced" with "cheek", as in "it's bare-faced cheek to ask for something you don't deserve"; but here, the term is connected with becoming accepted and respected as citizens of your adopted country.

The fifth stanza is a celebration of success and of the assimilation of the materialistic values of Tony Blair's Britain of the 1990s. It has stopped raining, nor is it too hot; so the immigrant family can enjoy its champagne and its heritage as well as its hard-earned commercial success. There is grammatical and linguistic awkwardness here, which shows that one hurdle still applies, however much the immigrant wants to be assimilated; the most difficult thing is not adapting to new customs and a new way of life, but tuning in to the nuances of grammar.

Just as the poem began with a linguistically clumsy title (it should, strictly, be "we have come to Dover" or "we are coming to Dover"), "my love and I" should be "my love and me"; "sundry others" should be "significant others"; "Blair'd" is not a verb; "beeswax'd" should be "polished" because cars are not made of wood; "crash clothes" should be "flash clothes"; and "lingoes" and "charged glasses" are an amusing attempt to appropriate upper-class terminology.

One of the lines of "Rule, Britannia" is "Thy cities shall with commerce shine"; this poem celebrates the contribution of the immigrant to the fulfilling of that patriotic vision, two hundred and fifty years later. Therefore, the poem is asking us who owns patriotism? At what point does an immigrant become as British as someone who has lived here all their life?

In Arnold's poem, the cliffs are not dirty and crumbling, but "glimmering and vast"; the sea is calm, and the air is sweet, not reeking of diesel fumes. He goes on to lament the loss, or erosion, of "Faith", which is the self-belief or confidence of the British nation. He says that the world which we regard as "a land of dreams" is actually dark, confused and full of strife. He is ambiguous about whether this dark conflict zone is the world beyond Britain, or Britain itself.

The meaning of "Dover Beach" is that if we lose confidence in ourselves, our dreams will turn to melancholy and misery; the remedy is to "be true to one another". Nagra interprets the "one another" to include everyone who comes to the shores of Britain. The unshakeable resilience of the immigrant contributes to the wider well-being of our society, as well as being measurable by their personal successes and achievements.

The language in Nagra's poem has such enthusiasm for all things British- such resilience- that you cannot help smiling when you read it. This is one of several poems in the collection you are studying which draws our attention to the need to be open to cultural influences very different from our own—the poems by Burnside, Doshi, Flynn, Heaney and Padel would all be useful comparisons.

Sean O'Brien   Fantasia on a Theme of James Wright

O'Brien is a poet who lives in Newcastle- on-Tyne, has an interest in railways, and is fascinated by the relationship between the past and the present, not in a nostalgic sense, but in a comparative one.

Those preoccupations come together in this poem, which is located at Killingworth. Killingworth was the site of a coal mine – the deepest mine in the world in 1882- and the locomotive engineer George Stephenson worked there as a young man. In the 1960s the mine was built over; Northumberland County Council facilitated the construction of a large new town, built in a contemporary architectural style. Their aspirations for the type of society this would create were not wholly achieved. West Moor and Palmersville were the sites of individual pits.

The title is less easily investigated. The American poet James Arlington Wright (1927-1980) was interested in the post- industrial landscapes of the American West, in the disenfranchised, and in the transcendent human spirit.

The other reference which needs to be understood is Hedley's "Coming Home". Hedley was a realist painter who grew up in Newcastle; this painting is in the city's Laing Art Gallery. It depicts two miners walking home from a shift at the mine. The older one is grey and bearded and carries a lamp. The younger man is carrying a pickaxe.

The poem includes one very unusual word-"noyade"-which refers to execution without a weapon, specifically by drowning.

The poem is full of references to water- rivers/ pools/ flooding/ ocean/ rush of water- and death by drowning was a constant hazard for miners in deep mines.

The poem, which is located where a huge housing estate has been superimposed on a huge mine, is executing the history, or at least the cultural awareness of the state of mind and values of the miner, so that the noise and memories of the mining era, and its class divisions, are buried beneath modern housing (materialism), even if the mining heritage is not completely out of mind.

O'Brien juxtaposes the dead and the living. The dead (miners) are still singing "inside the earth". The fact that they are dead is only established in the last two stanzas, which contrast them with "the living". The miners are in the first line of the poem, and throughout the first five stanzas. It is only when we reach line 14 that we start to wonder whether they are real, or some surreal memory from the past, jostling for a place in the present.

There is a focus in the language of the poem on words which we associate with death and its rituals- stones/black/ black-braided/prayers/ dead/ darkness/ dust/ down/earth/ underground/ lamentation/ inherit/ estate. The dead are below ground, the living above; the dead miners, and their way of life is, though, "immortalized- but "by want" i.e. by the lack of possessions, the lack of labour-saving technology, the absence of safety. The identity they were so proud of- the terraced houses, the outside toilets, the danger, the village culture- have been topped by the economic and social, urban vision of the 1960s and beyond.

The poem is in nine stanzas of three lines each; something interesting is happening in stanza 5 which is at the heart of the poem. The "tiny corridors of the immense estate" could be either/ both the mine shafts, where the prints might be pinned up as a token of good luck and a safe return home, and the halls and passageways of the small modern council houses which the next generation now occupies above the mine, or "aloft".

These homes are contrasted with the miners' underground "long home", the coal seam, in stanza 3. Their way of life may be immortalized in some way, but "we hardly hear of them" because all mining activity has stopped here, as in so many other places- "matters are otherwise".

Once we understand that the miners underground are in fact "the dead inside the earth", the images in the first five stanzas change; these miners are bodies, buried in the underground rivers, in spaces which are being compressed as coal starts to re-form, and as the water table adjusts with thuds and explosions. There is no mention of it, but subsidence could, in time, lead to the falling of the future into the past!

There is ambiguity about the purpose of the "iron doors"; they lock the dead inside the mines, and they also prevent the living from entering. The poem also uses the image of the doors closing to signify the end of "prayers and lamentations" (for miners killed in accidents, or for the way of life of mining?); the end of the need for pragmatism (perhaps accepting that fatal accidents will happen); the end of "the long noyade/ of a class" of workers who prided themselves on their poverty; the end of the slow decline and extinction of dangerous hard physical labour.

The whole poem is in the present tense, apart from the switch to the future tense for the final two lines. The past is thus part of the continuous and continuing present. Its values are industrial, as opposed to post-industrial, but its heritage, as recorded in Hedley's painting, is still able to be seen everywhere; it is just that, as time goes on, you have to look a little harder for it. Mourning for a dangerous, hard and superannuated way of life is not the way of the living; but their way is not the way of the dead.

Ciaran O'Driscoll   Please Hold

This poem satirizes the repetitive, or robotic, phone menus we encounter when we try to contact banks, utility companies and other institutions.

It consists of 52 lines, of which the last three are detached. Look down the poem at the last word of each line- you will observe the close-range, dense repetition of single words. For example, in lines 6-18- a total of 13 lines- only five words feature (needs, robot, number, account, nothing).

The language is highly repetitive, to emphasise the repetitive and monotonous process of automated call answering menus; the word **say/s** appears 16 times, **robot** 11 times, **hold** and **please** and **wonderful** five times. The narrator shouts and screams with frustration, while "my wife says"- four times- that "this is the future"- that there is no possibility of rejecting this impersonal application of technology. She is calm, because she is reconciled to this facet of modern life.

His frustration explodes in the swear word he applies to Mozart's "Eine Kleine Nachtmusik", on its third repetition; this over-familiar serenade for string orchestra was one of the staple pieces of music whenever callers were put on hold in the 1980s. It is intended to be soothing, but it has the opposite effect on him. Nowadays, you will find call centres using a wider range of tunes!

Some elements in the poem are surreal. A robot does not say "wonderful" or "great", or cut off the call when screamed at; these are conversational techniques where two-way communication between two people is in progress. Neither can a robot transfer a caller to himself. Nor does the narrator have a translator.

The translator only appears towards the end of the poem, unlike the narrator, his wife and the robot. The translator seems to be a cynical but shrewd inner voice; it knows that your call is not important, or not sufficiently important to be answered with care and individual attention, and it asserts that the narrator should go "looting"- an unexpected, anarchic word denoting a rebellious and anti-social act. "Meet your needs" is an ironic business-speak phrase (line 48 echoes line 13).

"No options" in line 35 echoes the "countless options" of line 5, in an ironic way. The length and pattern of sentences becomes shorter and shorter, until it becomes meaninglessly robotic in the closing lines. There are 42 sentences in 52 lines. If we exclude the sentence which occupies lines 11 to 16, there are 41 sentences in 46 lines. In 27 of these sentences, the narrator is being spoken to- either instructed by the robot or the translator, or told, by his wife, how the world is.

In lines 37-42 and lines 50-52 the narrator's thoughts are interpolated between the request, or polite imperative, to "please hold". The flat tone is clever and amusing, because, in the end, we cannot be sure what is being said and what is merely being thought. The extreme brevity of the sentences dramatizes the way in which communication is closed down.

Ruth Padel   You, Shiva, and My Mum

This poem consists of twelve stanzas of three lines each, with the even stanzas indented. It comprises a series of eight questions, answered by the final words "Yes. Tell that." By this point, though, the tale has already been told!

Three characters appear in the poem, in the reverse of the order in which they appear in the title of the poem.

"My mum" is an indomitable woman aged 80, a religious sceptic, whose determination to attend the wedding of her last unmarried son surpassed the discomforts of old age, 100 degree heat and monsoons, riding on the back of a motor bike on a hilly path blocked by sleeping water buffalo, her dislike of ostentatiousness and superstition, and fording a river. As if that is not enough, she then had to climb up a rock-slide, barefoot.

If we were to remove the interrogative words in lines 1, 10, 16, 20, 26 and 32, we would have a straightforward narrative, but a little of the sense of incredulous wonder and admiration would be missing. These interrogative words take a narrative which is told in the past tense, and they bring it into the present, making it more immediate and visual in the process.

The elderly mother dominates the poem via a series of descriptive images (**just as in the Adam Thorpe poem**). Her daughter-in-law is waiting, in lines 6-9, highly decorated, in a cave at a shrine in a forest- an inaccessible place, reached only by motorbike and on foot, up a dangerous and slippery jungle path, and then across boulders.

The god Shiva finds a place in lines 20-25 and 28-29; the rituals which go with him are part of the frills the mother dislikes, but she is careful not to offend local custom, and shows respect by bowing to his statue. But Shiva here is merely a statue, kept company by some flowers and plants and "his little bull of stone".

These statuettes have no energy; all the dynamism is with the unstoppable elderly mother.

The addressee of the poem- "you"- appears belatedly in line 32, to burst the bubble of pride the narrator feels at having the mother she does. The narrator does not regard her mother as miraculous, but she awaits a reunion with the "you" in the poem, and its whispered intimacy, as "the miracle".

Ruth Padel confirms (on her website) that she is the narrator of this poem, and that she accompanied her mother on this hazardous expedition, and was indeed looking forward to being able to return home.

Just as Shiva has a small place in the poem, there is a small space for the formality and tradition of rhyme- monsoon/moon/noon; face/place; Hindu/you. But the mother, with her boundless energy and her lack of superstition, will not be constrained by the normal limitations of life, and so the poem will not be subjected to a formal and conventional rhyme scheme- only to a few nods, a bow in its general direction.

In a land of powerful, primitive and competing religious traditions, the maternal head of the family navigates all the obstacles, to see the last of her sons married- thus forging new links, or, as Ruth Padel says, "making connections over continents, time zones, families".

This theme has something in common with John Burnside's poem "History", and George Szirtes' "Song", in that the impact of actions and events is not limited to the narrow place where they happen; continents are inter-connected, just as injustices throughout history and all over the world are inter-connected- by the need to end them.

George Szirtes   Song

Szirtes came to Britain as a Hungarian refugee in the late 1950s. He has written, in this poem, about the latent power of even the smallest voice of (political) protest. The dedication to Helen Suzman sets a political context; she was a white, Jewish woman who had a long career as a Member of Parliament in South Africa. In opposing apartheid, she defied the entrenched attitudes of white South Africans long before any organised protests had begun.

Her role was therefore as a proto-protestor (or, to borrow Heaney's term, an incubator!). She was the "feather tip"- the smallest possible, and unlikeliest imaginable source of imbalance and rebalance.

In calling the poem simply "Song", and using such simple language and such a simple rhyme scheme,

Szirtes is alluding to William Blake's "Songs of Innocence and Experience", which draw attention to the victimised and to abuses of power in the early 1800s. Szirtes is pointing out that, 200 years later, the need to defy imbalances of power is still just as valid- and it still demands courage in the face of apparently hopeless odds (stanza 3).

Stanzas 1 and 4 are almost identical, so that they could be mistaken as confirming the status quo and as standing for continuity- the more so, as the rhyme scheme is AAAA, and because of the almost perfect replication, in the final stanza, of the position at the start of the poem. However, the tiny alteration- replacing the word "till" with "then"- is subversive because it changes everything; it makes change on a bigger-even massive- scale inevitable. This small and subtle change confirms the argument in stanza 4! The smallest of changes can lead to world-changing change; as in the poem, so in the wider world.

This pairing of stanzas 1 and 6 naturally leads us to examine stanzas 2 and 5 for similarities and differences. They share a rhyme scheme ABABCC. Stanza 5 imports some of its line-ends – *hall* comes from stanza 2, and *does* and *buzz* come from stanza 1. It also borrows hands, air, and breaking from stanza 2, but with adjustments. *A lot of small hands* becomes *hands, however small* (there are fewer of them and they are smaller). Making the air vibrate becomes filling the air. Sinking becomes lifting. The momentum is with the tiny resources. Instead of the sound of a plate being broken, we hear "the buzz of the broken" as they adjust the balance of society (a monstrous hall, and a sinking ship).

This leaves stanzas 3 and 4, which stand out because they are not in italics. The stanzas in italics are aspirational but provisional- they speak of what can potentially happen. The solid stanzas 3 and 4 state what appear to be presented as proven truths, by relating the argument they put forward to the past and to actual events.

The phrase "certain people" means not only identifiable people but also people who have the certainty to believe in the need for change, and work for it (such as Helen Suzman). The italicised dream is affirmed in the two central stanzas- they say that such hopes have been realised "time and again".

We talk about "the heavy lifting" as the groundwork necessary to achieve a successful outcome (e.g. the forwards in a rugby team wearing down the opposition so that the backs can score tries later in the game). The language here is of lifting heavy objects, and of shifting the (im)balance to achieve a new equilibrium- levers (twice), fulcrum (twice), tip, balance, heavy and weight (four times), and earthmoving (line 22).

That this is an imbalance of power, not weight, is clear from another group of words- crushed (line 15), hushed (16), oppose (14), object (20) and break/broken (8,16,25).

The poem itself enacts the rebalancing of which it speaks. The voice of Helen Suzman, and replacing the word *till* in line 4 with the word *then* in line 32, are the pale feather tip which causes the ship of the unjust state to overbalance. Shaking the wall leads to making the Earth move.

Stanzas 3 and 4 present the power of social protest almost as a physical law of the universe, as though history is the scientific proof of the theorem (line 21).

The anthemic repetition of key words and lines simplifies the argument and makes the poem more like a song. These repetitions set "nothing" against "something", five times. The emphasis on action comes out in the use of the word "does", five times- always at the end of a line, and, naturally, as the last word of the poem.

Reading the poem, we are prompted to think of social revolutions in different eras and different parts of the world- the abolition of slavery, the human rights movement in the USA, the collapse of apartheid, and of communism; Tiananmen Square; votes for women; the Russian Revolution; the French Revolution- and to ask ourselves how they began, and what the world would have been like if no-one had stood up for minorities and the oppressed.

The poem is a song or celebration, rather than an elegy for Helen Suzman, because it is a celebration of the concept that there is an immutable law, a **great fate**, that against the **weight** of social injustice, the **plate**s will **vibrate**, and a rebalancing change will set things right.

The narrator in Fanthorpe's poem faces a personal, not a political, struggle. She, too, insists on being heard- the monstrous fabric and the monstrous hall both seem all-powerful, but throwing away the servant's tray, or breaking a plate, sets off the act of protest which will, by the end of each poem, change the dynamics of society.

Adam Thorpe   On her Blindness

Like Alan Jenkins' "Effects", this poem documents a son's feelings (for Jenkins, of guilt) once his mother has died.

Thorpe's poem is in twenty-two unrhymed couplets and one final line; a form no other poem in your collection uses. The ostensible subject- the handicap of his mother's blindness- is dealt with in a way which leaves blank spaces between the couplets. The poem is full of enjambment, and it would be easier to read if it were set out in four-line stanzas, or even (as Jenkins does) in a single stanza. This layout, in practice, creates a mild visual obstacle, or impairment, for the reader- it succeeds in making the act of reading harder than usual.

It also prompts us to "read between the lines", and acknowledge that there are strong feelings- especially on her side- behind the black comedy with which the issue of blindness is treated in this family; it may be hard to talk about, or mitigate, but we should at least try.

The references to Paris and Berkshire indicate that this is an autobiographical poem and that Thorpe is dealing here with his own family history.

The poem uses the noun "vision" to mean both his mother's (lack of) sight, and the narrator's (lack of) insight into the difficulty of living with blindness. Despite his mother's frankness in lines 12-14, he cannot solve the problem; his father makes her tendency to bump into walls into a joke.

This male larking about over a serious issue extends to the terms of childhood play- dodgem, new toy, slide, seesaw (line 23!)- and the humour is a masculine way of dealing with their impotence to help, and their reluctance to talk about her feelings with her. The narrator feels "locked in" to a pattern of evasion; that forces her to pretend she does not feel resourceless (21-22) even after we know that she does feel desperate (12-14). The effect of her words on the reader is more powerful than their impact on her son.

The poem is "darker" than the black humour would like to make it. There is a cluster of words to do with death- coffin, dying, the void, last, hell, sightless, bump myself off, finished, fall, sink, nothing, and, of course, the final words of the poem- "the end".

The language of evasion is also prominent- in the sense of the content of lines 2, 3, 14, 16, 20-22, 28-33, 38, and in the words forget/forgetting, hide, ignore, pretend/pretended.

The narrator is "locked-in" (line 16); locked-in syndrome is a form of paralysis which makes communication of any kind virtually impossible. She is locked into her blindness, "blank", "sightless", but his handicap is really almost as debilitating and damaging. He is trying to turn a blind eye to her suffering as a result of her very real blindness.

It is sad but true that it takes a death to bring out the extent of the dysfunction in many families. The direct speech in this poem gives the narrator's mother an admirable resilience; there is no self-pity in it, which is just as well, since the narrator lists her potential and actual mishaps without any tangible sympathy. This comes to a head in the final five lines, where he tells us the dead have to stop pretending they can see! His mother had only pretended to be able to see her grandchildren's toys and drawings because they were thrust at her, unthinkingly (lines 23-28). She has always been much more sensitive to her family's feelings than they have been to hers.

Ironically, his mother had never pretended about the despair she felt. The people who need to stop pretending are the narrator and his father; they should stop pretending that blindness is funny.

The narrative presents a series of images of the mother's difficulties- being unable to feed herself, bumping into walls, admiring the drawings and toys she cannot see, driving a big old car when she is a danger to herself and others, thinking she is looking at a television when it is behind her, and finally sitting "too weak to move". Strikingly, no-one helps her on any of these occasions.

The narrator thinks that she chose to pretend to ignore her impairment (lines 21, 42-43). In fact, she was coping with it as best she could, without any help from the (male) members of her own family.

She died two weeks before the poem is written. The narrator cannot quite accept that she is dead; he and his family are left "to believe she was watching, somewhere"- ironically, as watching, while she was blind, was the last thing she would be able to do.

The poem is a dramatic monologue. True to form, its narrator accidentally discloses his own inadequacies- a lack of care, a lack of empathy- which may often characterise the relationship between adult sons and their mothers, once they have left home.

Apart from reminding us that men may generally make mediocre carers, this poem differs from "Effects" in that Thorpe's speaker does not appear to regret his past behaviour (yet); he regards what he "replied" and "told" her as good enough, though "inadequate". There is no sense that he sees any wrongs in his own attitudes which need to be put right; but perhaps that would come later, once the irreversibility of her death has impressed itself on him.

The narrator claims that we may reasonably refuse to acknowledge the effects of disability on those who suffer it (lines 3-4). As readers, we know that exactly the reverse is true. Because the narrator feels neither grief nor loss, we distance ourselves from him, and our sympathy fastens on to his late mother.

Like the protagonist in Fanthorpe's "A Minor Role", she refuses to make a fuss and sustains the background music of civility. It is unfortunate for her that we cannot choose our family, but at least the poet can treat his narrator ironically- rather as **Andrew Motion does, in "From the Journal of a Disappointed Man"**.

Tim Turnbull   Ode on a Grayson Perry Urn

This poem is a modern response to Keats' famous "Ode on a Grecian Urn", from which the most quoted extract is:

"Beauty is truth, truth beauty- that is all/ Ye know on earth, and all ye need to know".

Keats' Ode comprises five stanzas of ten lines each, in iambic pentameters. Each stanza starts with a rhyme pattern of ABAB; lines 5-10 then offer variations on a CDECDE pattern.

Keats describes (and eulogises) a Greek urn, decorated with Gods and mortals in the countryside, enjoying a "wild ecstasy" of pursuit and escape- an orgiastic party out of doors, but one in which the quietness is unravished, and pretty girls remain unkissed.

The first scene on the urn immortalises Spring and youth; a second scene depicts a priest bringing a calf to a ritual sacrifice. The poem ends with the idea that when we, the readers of Keats, are all old, and other people have other troubles, this urn will still stand as a timeless monument to the beauty of the young people who inspired it and whom it depicts.

Turnbull replicates the form of Keats' poem very closely, but the tone of his Ode is much more down-to-earth and it has a harder edge. The narrative voice is observant, discriminating and ironic, where Keats' was sentimental and lyrical. Turnbull calls the Grayson Perry urn (which you can see, on the cover illustration of your anthology) "you garish crock"- hardly an expression of admiration. Keats' quietness, silence and slow time have nothing to do with today's "youth culture", which Turnbull's sardonic narrator debunks, even as he admires its energy.

The new Ode substitutes the contemporary equivalent at each stage of Keats' poem, as it refurbishes it and brings it up to date. The Grayson Perry urn is decorated with fast, over-powered, turbo-charged cars and the words "money, power, status, God, death, sex"- the gods, or preoccupations, of young people today? The contrast is extreme, between Keats' rural calm and Turnbull's noise and smoke, and between Keats' idolising of the urn he sees, and Turnbull's description of his own so-called inspiration as cheap and casual.

The second stanza replaces Keats' soft melodic pan pipes with the throaty roar of hatchbacks (the sporty Ford Fiesta XR2, perhaps, which was seen as a status symbol on council estates in the 1980s, and caricatured as the toy of Essex boys chasing Essex girls) and with "garage" or house music. Keats' assertion that the girls on the urn he writes about will not be kissed survives in this stanza, but we find the idea mildly incredulous, in the context of a youth "culture" driven by the gods of sex and power. Indeed, Turnbull's "games of chlamydia roulette" acknowledge frankly that the chastity in Keats' Ode has no place here.

In fact, Turnbull cleverly exploits and conflates the language of fast cars and the language of sex. The car/roads lexis comprises motors, motorways, lanes, wheels, tarmac, charged, cars, turbo, throb, tuned, hatchbacks, fired, tyres, traction, continent, burn-outs, pull, breaking, skid, flip, speed, bass, box, buff, squeals, screech, imported, race, alloy, highway, estates, verge, deflated, raw, pumped, head, fired.

Some of these words have sexual connotations too- throb, pull, flip, squeals, screech, buff, verge (virgin?), pumped, deflated, head- and other sexual lexis is knocked, gyratory, thong, throaty, nervous, night, screech, crude, chlamydia, expose, bed, beauty, pulsing, juice. In fact, Turnbull translates the non-penetrative "panting....passion.......tongue" in Keats' third stanza into a series of self-confessedly "crude" allusions to oral sex in his corresponding lines (26-30). This activity risks chlamydia- a different sort of burning from Keats' "burning forehead", and a different sort of "head" altogether.

Speed, ecstasy and grass (cannabis- a different grass from Keats' rural landscape) fuel the scene in Turnbull's poem with drugs. This is an imaginative elaboration on the "original" urn.

In the fourth stanza of Keats' poem, the whole population of the "little town" comes out to watch the slaughter of the calf, so that the town is empty and quiet. Turnbull populates his fourth stanza with a crowd of cheerleaders; the religious ritual is not the killing of an animal, but extremely noisy street-racing, to the accompaniment of an audience drinking strong cider.

Keats' final stanza says that contemplating the urn makes us think of eternity, and we feel "cold" when we realise that the urn will outlive us, as a timeless celebration of the beauty of being young. Turnbull, too, winds the clock forward, to "millennia hence" and an age where the sun is "a little colder"; he says that "future poets" who look at the Grayson Perry urn (as Keats had looked at the Greek urn) will say, not that truth and beauty are the same thing, but that neither is objectively measurable. Living a "free" life means not being concerned with artistic notions of objective truth or aesthetic beauty; those things are subjective, relative and personal to us.

We have a phrase "Beauty is in the eye of the beholder", meaning that we respond to what we see or perceive as beautiful. Turnbull takes this further; the phrase "in the gift of the beholder" emphasises even more strongly the idea that our notion of beauty is subjective, not objective. His poem therefore ends with a final debunking (or updating) of the Keatsian view of the world; the ancient Greeks represented their concerns about God, sex and death in their own way, and we do in ours- very differently.

If you read Turnbull's poem without comparing it closely, line by line, or at least stanza by stanza, with Keats' Ode, it seems irritated, energetic, unfocused, and, in places, contradictory. However, in the context of a proper comparison, the Turnbull Ode is richer, more humorous and humane than we would otherwise understand it to be.

The key to the poem is therefore the intertextuality; a dimension of analysis which also applies, in a different way, to Motion's "From the Journal of Disappointed Man", and, less strongly, to the poems in the anthology by Ciaran Carson and Daljit Nagra.

Turnbull's linguistic humour lies in the colloquial approach he adopts- kids, donut, crap, crock, buff, geezer are the language of the street, not of the high-minded, lyrical poetic form, the Ode. The drink, drugs and sex in his poem bring an element of realism to the impressionistic sentimentality in Keats' poem. The legacy of the Industrial Revolution means that the new Ode has to be urban /suburban instead of rural/pastoral. If Keats is painting in watercolours, Turnbull is in oils, and like Jackson Pollock.

Turnbull's poem seems to come from a different world; but it shares with Keats a sense of the energy and optimism of each generation of adolescents and young adults- the momentary sense that we can live intensely, for the moment, and that we will never grow old.

This idea that human experience over long spans of time has not changed very much emerges, too, **in the poems by Carson, Boyle, Heaney and O'Brien.**

Part Two: Applying Your Understanding.

Your Essay at AS level

The AS poetry essay carries 24 marks; this means that you should spend no more than 40 minutes answering it.

The task is designed to test your knowledge of poetic form, language and conventions.

The assessment criteria which apply are-

AO1 - articulate an informed, personal and creative response to literary texts using associated concepts and terminology, and coherent, accurate written expression

AO2 - analyse ways in which meanings are shaped in literary texts

AO4 - explore connections across literary texts.

Students often ask if it is best to concentrate their learning on their 'favourite' or more easily understandable poems. However, there can be no way of knowing which of the 28 poems will be chosen – so I would not advise it. Clearly, some poems lend themselves to being compared with several others, making them superficially more useful (meaning you are more likely to be able to have something meaningful to say, whatever the printed poem is). But many of the poems have more subtle and more interesting common ground just below their surfaces.

Here are two sample essays, which should help you to gauge what your own essays might include.

Essay 1

Compare the treatment of internationalism in George Szirtes' "Song" and one other poem.

Szirtes dedicates his poem to Helen Suzman, who was in a small minority, as an anti-apartheid MP in South Africa, from 1953 to 1989, and was in an even smaller one, being a woman and Jewish.

The very simple rhyme scheme and repetitive structure of the poem allude to the "songs" of William Blake; this reference reminds us that innocence and experience offer us a very simple way to express what is repressed, and to give a voice to the disenfranchised. Szirtes makes injustice concrete by representing it as a "weight", and he builds a subtly different balance by changing one word- a single brick in the wall- in stanza 6, which otherwise repeats and reinforces stanza 1. The rhymes of weight with vibrate/ plate/fate/great contrast with the isolated and delicate "pale feather tip", which tips the balance in favour of the crushed/hushed, with their tiny hands and the tiny buzzing noise they make in the distance.

Stanza 3 links non-aggressive political protest in South Africa with its historical antecedents- the abolition of slavery and the civil rights movement in the USA come to mind, but there is no prescriptive list. The reference to a sinking ship (line 10) leads us to understand that the creaking ship of an oppressive state is weak, however strong it seems, because it is undemocratic.

The poem is built from wide contrasts (nothing/something, small/great) and a tight rhyme scheme – five stanzas ABABCC framed by two AAAA stanzas. The phrase "certain people" refers both to people like Helen Suzman, and to any person who has moral certainty- both can make the Earth move. Within a system of government which is broken because it breaks and crushes dissent, even the smallest resistance can be the means of lifting this oppressive weight- that is a law of history and of physics.

It is only the dedication to Suzman which connects the content of the poem with South Africa. Szirtes is universalising the power of protest, arguing that it applies as a law of (human) nature in all circumstances. The refrain "Nothing happens until something does" emphasises the difference between passive acceptance and the first tiny stirring of resistance, from which earth-changing shifts in balance develop. The oppressive weight is like "the heart", in two ways; as protests gathers force, the heart "begins to lift", with a sense of relief, optimism and joy, and the weight of being crushed begins to be lifted too. The cleverest thing in the poem is the way in which the minute change in stanza 6 from stanza 1 enacts the "distant buzz" at the moment when something starts to happen.

Szirtes uses a small number of very simple, unspecific images to convey the essential issues in his poem. There are no identifiable people, only "a lot of small hands", a feather, a voice, a plate breaking , and a digger or earth-moving equipment.

Doshi's "The Deliverer" explores the international implications of infanticide in rural India. Unlike Szirtes' narrator, who (like Blake's narrator) seems to be the voice of the bard, Doshi's narrator is hard to identify; all we know is that he/she is the child of a woman who went to Kerala to rescue the most damaged child she could find. The fact that the child who is the subject of the poem can remember the day she was born implies, perhaps, that the narrator is that same child.

As with Szirtes, Doshi uses the outer sections of her poem to present the issue of the rejection and infanticide of female children and those otherwise judged defective ("crippled or dark or girls"). The convent sister has a range of shocking anecdotes; it is clear from the third section of the poem that those early memories cannot be erased in the consciousness of the child who survives or escapes- the "heap of others" is similar to being "covered in garbage", a form of abandonment motivated by deliberate cruelty.

There are no men in this poem, until the last line, or the last three lines; instead, there are references just to female personae- sister/mother/girls/this girl/woman to woman/mothers. The rejection of defective babies is a cultural issue. It is hard to blame the mothers, who "trudge home" to become routinely pregnant over and over again.

The second section of the poem changes the setting to America, and shows us a rather hysterical civic desire to save these children. There is much emoting ("we couldn't stop crying"), but it is futile to pretend that a satisfactory bond can form between children and "parents" in and from different continents. The urge to help seems to come from groups of citizens, not from the policymakers in government.

The narrator's mother is one of the group of parents at the airport; it appears that a number of adoptive families await the arrival of a shipment of Indian babies, whose fetishes and psychological distress they are unaware of. Stanza 8 suggests that the adoptive parents cannot cope with this, and they, too, pass the child on, so that the sense of abandonment is merely reinforced in the final 9 lines.

Unlike Szirtes, Doshi does not affirm that there is an international solution to the suffering her poem addresses. Thus, there is no rhyme scheme, and the tone is elegiac , not positive. The images are like the poem's video tapes- a series of photographic snapshots of oppression and abandonment.

Just as Szirtes gives his poem a global dimension, through the device of "the very same tune that has been sung/ time and again", Doshi puts the well-intentioned but ill-informed and superficial people of the USA in the middle of her poem. Clearly, their compassion is not an effective solution to the problem; choosing the most damaged children you can find and "rescuing" them does not resolve the trauma of their origins. The reader is left to reflect that aid driven by compassion is a sticking plaster on a deep wound which is cultural in origin, and not susceptible to this sort of treatment.

Essay 2

Compare the treatment of immaturity in Motion's "From the Journal of a Disappointed Man" and one other poem.

Motion takes the title of his poem from an earlier text by Barbellion, a naturalist who had written of his struggle with self-absorption and his sense of how insignificant his own life was.

Motion's narrator turns a non-event into a poem of eleven stanzas of four lines each. His elevated language (paraphernalia, ruminative, monosyllables, indifferent, trajectory, majesty) is pretentious, and designed to draw attention to himself. The last words of the poem – "and me, of course"- sum up his ambition to put himself at the centre of the stage. The eleven stanzas seek to construct a grand architecture out of a wooden block.

The narrator's personal insignificance is matched by the insignificance of the poem's narrative- nothing happens at all. He tries to infuse meaning into the act of standing on a ladder, or gazing into the water. There is a comical irony here- the workmen are not "like a mystic"; nor are they heroic, however much the narrator seeks to imbue them with these qualities. The "secret problem", or "great difficulty", is a misreading of the workmen's indolence.

The narrator is both paranoid- he thinks the men were "ignoring me"- and a repetitive bore ("as I said"). All of his hyperbolic language (discovered/massive/very/all/great/monsters/finally/ abandoned /eclipse/suddenly) cannot bridge the gap between the ordinariness of the scene and his ambitions for it.

The poem is both a narrative and a dramatic monologue- true to this form, the speaker reveals more about himself than he means to, and none of it is flattering. The end of the poem leaves us with the comical idea of the pile suspended in mid-air, and the narrator similarly suspended, between his delusions of self-importance and the pathetic reality of his life.

O'Driscoll's "Please Hold" likewise presents a narrator who is unhappy and frustrated. The use of repetition as a substitute for rhyme demonstrates his rigid thinking, and also the repetitive cycle of call-centre telephone menus. He shouts and screams, while the robot calmly gives him instructions- the phrase "says the robot" appears five times. The narrator's wife repeatedly points out to him that this is the future (six times). As the cycle of repetitions tightens towards the end of the poem, and as the rhyme of hold/old/cold/told becomes dictatorial and controlling, the narrator loses his autonomy. He has no influence.

While the narrator satirises his telephone experience, he is not really detached from it at all. He wants to speak to "someone real", but there re twelve uses of the noun "robot", plus one appearance of the adjective "robotic". His resistance continues; it is captured forcefully in the swear word in line 40.

While there is a clever elision in the poem between what is actually said and what the narrator thinks or feels is said, the purpose of the call seems to be to transfer money from his account; in the end, he is reduced to a desperate plan to meet his needs "by looting"- an anti-social and criminal act. This is hyperbolic, and its roots lie is the narrator's inability to see the world as it is (and to adjust to technology). His agitation and fury is amusing because it is futile; his wife's calm brushing off of all his protests is similar to the robot's.

We expect poems about growing up to be full of optimism. We expect poems about adulthood to be full of realism. Both of these narrators are inadequate, because they lack the maturity to adjust to the world they live in. Both protest against what they see as a conspiracy to ignore them or deny them what they need (meaningful human contact). While this may be indicative of a mid-life crisis for the middle-class male, neither poem evokes sympathy for its narrator. Their foibles raise a wry smile. Both poems use a narrative style to convey their narrators' preoccupations. The reader feels that both narrators really need to get a life.

Essay practice, and identifying themes

Once you are familiar with all of the 28 poems, you will begin to see thematic connections between them.

It may help to think first in terms of the contrasts or tensions the poems set up and explore, between opposite experiences, positions or views. See if you can locate these themes in one or more of the poems, and add your own topics to the list as you go along-

Assertiveness/deference

Cultural differences/ terrorism

Unawareness/ awareness (of self and others)

Independence/ dependence

Maturity/ immaturity

Parochialism/ internationalism

Responsibility/ irresponsibility

Confidence/lack of confidence

Inexperience/ experience

Ignorance/ knowledge

Feelings of guilt/ innocence

Emigration/ immigration

Vulnerability/ sense of control

Domestic or family world/ wide world

Subjectivity/ objectivity

What is lost/ what is found

Significance/ insignificance

(Female) dependence/ empowerment

Youth/ age

Having a voice/ being voiceless

Being confident/ lacking confidence

Expediency/ moral values

Which poems make good comparisons

Finally, here is a list of themes or topics in each poem. You can extract a shared theme to enable you to make comparisons between the poems, wherever one of these themes is common ground. This would be a very good way of practising the selection and comparing of poems as you prepare for your exam!

Agbabi   Feminine compliance/ gratification/ power in relationships

Armitage   Male aggression/ feminism/ gratification/ violence

Barber   Death of mother/ childhood/
parenthood/ memories of childhood

Boland   Parenthood/ economic repression
(of women)/ mothers and children

Boyle   Becoming adult/innocence/
unawareness/ vulnerability/ unknowable future

Burnside   Parenthood/ terrorism/ anxiety/
internationalism

Carson   Internationalism/ violence/
objectivity

Copus   Growing up/ unknowable future/
parents and children

Doshi   Infanticide/ internationalism/
cultural differences/ migration

Duffy   Growing up/ memories of
childhood/ independence/ empowerment of women

Duhig   Violence/ objectivity/ death of wife/
supernatural/ guilt

Dunmore   Memories of childhood/ growing up

Fanthorpe   Deference/ suffering/ finding a
voice/ growing up/ protest

Feaver   Violence/ power/ gratification/
supernatural

Flynn   Growing up/ awareness/ innocence/ childishness/ insignificance

Ford   Violence/ voicelessness/ guilt/ expediency

Heaney   The subconscious/ supernatural/ childishness/ growing up

Jenkins   Death of mother/ guilt/ childhood memories/ children and parents/ old age

Minhinnick   Adaptability/ supernatural/ history/ continuity of time

Morrissey   Children and parents/ growing up/ parenthood

Motion   Immaturity/ insignificance/ self-importance

Nagra   Migration/ cultural differences/ hostility/ growing up

O'Brien   Continuity of time and history/ economic change

O'Driscoll   Insignificance/ anger/ protest/ immaturity

Padel   Children and mothers/ family/ old age

Szirtes   Protest/ internationalism/ being voiceless/ power

Thorpe	Death of mother/ guilt/ growing up/ children and parents
Turnbull	Growing up/ change (cultural)/ time and continuity

Gavin Smithers is a private tutor, covering Broadway, Chipping Campden and the North Cotswolds. He has an English degree from Oxford University, and a passion for helping others to discover the joy and satisfaction of great literature.

And finally …if there's anything you're not sure about and your teacher can't help, contact the author – grnsmithers@hotmail.co.uk

Gavin's Guides are short books packed with insight. Their key aim is to help you raise your grade!

Understanding Arthur Miller's All My Sons.Understanding J.B. Priestley's An Inspector Calls. Understanding George Orwell's Animal Farm. Understanding William Golding's Lord of the Flies. Understanding Charles Dickens' Great Expectations. Understanding John Steinbeck's Of Mice and Men. Understanding Emily Dickinson's Set Poems. Understanding Edward Thomas' Set Poems. Understanding Harper Lee's To Kill A Mockingbird. Understanding Andrew Marvell's Cromwell & Eulogy Poems

CPSIA information can be obtained
at www.ICGtesting.com
Printed in the USA
LVOW04s2003070916
503615LV00022B/897/P